Using Other People's Money

How to invest in property

Second Edition

— VICKI WUSCHE —

Using Other People's Money How to invest in property

Second Edition

—— Vicki Wusche ——

Using Other People's Money: How to invest in property
© Vicki Wusche 2012
ISBN 978-1-909116-00-9
First published in 2010 by Vizzi Publishing

This second edition published in 2012 by SRA Books

Printed in the UK by TJ International, Padstow

Vicki Wusche
The Shed
St Peters Road
Uxbridge, UB8 3SB

Vicki@ThePropertyMermaid.com
Skype: Vicki.Wusche
www.ThePropertyMermaid.com
www.TheSourcersApprentice.com

Liability disclaimer

The information contained in this book has been gathered and collated from the experiences of the author. Every effort has been made to make sure the details are accurate. However, they are experiences and by that nature, and the fact that they have been gathered into a book, means that they will be in the past as you read this.

It is vital that you take this information and check its relevancy to your personal situation and to the market place right now. We have been through four of the most unprecedented years in the economy, all rulebooks have been torn up and no one knows what the future holds. It is the lessons of the present that carry us forward.

Please take this information, learn from the mistakes, benefit from the successes and, above all, carve your own future in the shape you desire. Deals are easy to find but hard to buy without finance; identify your personal sources of finance and build a cashflow portfolio now.

Contents

Foreword by Simon Zutshi

Vicki and I first met when I was speaking at a property event in 2010 and at the time she was considering sharing some of her property investing knowledge through the creation of an ebook. Vicki kindly shared with me her belief that many people find it difficult to invest in property because they think they have financial restraints, and thus the need for a book which would help people to understand how to make money work for them, instead of having to work for money!

During our conversation I suggested to Vicki that if she really wanted to spread her message to a lot of people, she should step up and print a physical book rather than an ebook. I am delighted that she rose to my challenge and *Using Other Peoples Money: How to invest in property* was

Simon Zutshi, Founder of PIN

first published in 2010. It was an immediate success, and all copies were sold out within the first 15 months, which has led to this second edition being brought to print.

The timing of this book is perfect, as in the current economic climate it is even more important to be creative in order to live the life you want. With this book you will take your first step and understand how to use money wisely, and how to view your finances from an investment perspective.

Vicki is an inspiration to us all through her savvy skills in business management, and how she has a perfect work life balance, enjoying many holidays under the water through her love of scuba diving. She is continuing to expand her work through mentoring and coaching sessions. I have observed Vicki's own development and have noticed how she really listens to her clients, and gets to the core of how they would like to live their life, before implementing key steps for them to follow to achieve success.

Vicki's second book was launched just recently and I hear there is a third on the way. Her trilogy of books is likely to draw the reader on a journey through finding the money to start investing with, to how to make more money from those properties, and finally helping their families get long lasting financial freedom.

And finally, I am delighted that Vicki has also started speaking at property events. It is fantastic to see another successful female investor speaking at events, in an industry, which let's be honest, can sometimes appear to be male dominated. If you notice that Vicki is going to be speaking at an event near you, make sure you take the opportunity to hear her tell her story in person.

Simon Zutshi

Author of Amazon No 1 best seller *Property Magic*

Founder of PIN, the property investors network

About Vicki Wusche and this revised edition

Property investment is a strategic game that requires the investor to be constantly aware of the changing economic climate around them. This second edition of *Using Other People's Money: How to invest in property* will recap on certain elements of the first edition; other chapters have been radically rewritten, completely rejecting some of the previous strategies in light of the current economic climate.

Any business environment, if providing opportunities, will by nature be dynamic. When I wrote the first edition of this book in 2010, the previous two years had been mad and chaotic with everything that existing investors knew thrown into

Vicki Wusche, The Property Mermaid

the air. Many investors spent time and money 'trying' to find 'new' ways of investing. In fact, they were just avoiding the reality of the situation. Banks no longer wanted to lend 100% of the loan amount. We had to find a new way of doing business. The first edition reviewed those strategies through my experience and those of colleagues, in an effort to make sense of that new world and all the ideas being developed. This second edition adds another 18 months' experience into the mix.

During the past two years, I have continued to buy investment properties for myself and clients. I have worked with other investors (some new and others very experienced) to look at how we can easily make more money from property – this, in turn, prompted my second book, *Make More Money from Property: From investor thinking to a business mindset*.

So, why rewrite this book? Because there is still a demand from investors, new and experienced, to learn what is working well and what is not. And so there should be. Because without continual professional and business development, our portfolios would stop providing us with the financial freedom that we desire!

Let me start by explaining how I started my journey into property investment, so you can see that everything in this book is possible. The difference between the two editions (apart from the new ebook format that is available) is that two years later I have yet more experience to offer.

In the following chapters I will explain the tools and strategies you need to be successful and why identifying your own sources of personal finance is crucial to building a cashflowing portfolio.

First, to introduce myself

Vicki scuba diving

I am sometimes known as 'The Property Mermaid'. This is because buying property and scuba diving are my two main passions. It is, in fact, a little more complex than that… my desire to scuba dive all the warm waters of the world has always been a key goal and driving force in my life – even before property. Once I understood how money worked, the concept of leverage, and subsequently the advantage of leveraging other people's money, I was able to create a business and lifestyle that let me indulge both passions – property investment and scuba diving.

I am truly fortunate, grateful and happy. Property investment can enable you to live the life of your dreams. When you understand my journey, I hope that this book can open the door to financial freedom through a property portfolio and to a world you never thought of. Our biggest challenge is to overcome years of conditioning through our parents and school that encourages us to get a job, buy a house and live happily ever after. Yes, I want that too, but the difference is that I have recognised that I need to invest my money and make it work alongside and for me to achieve that dream. Not hope that a government pension will keep me warm in my old age!

The Mermaid

I always wanted to be like Jacques Cousteau, the great underwater explorer and adventurer. As a child I was always swimming in local pools or the sea. Finally, at 17, I discovered a scuba diving school. Unfortunately, I also discovered that I am a fair-weather diver and, as my club dived mostly in the UK, I never did fully qualify. Nevertheless, at 17 years old I could haul a six-foot man two lengths of an Olympic-sized swimming pool, pull him out of the water and resuscitate him!

One of the disadvantages of being human and breathing air is the need to occasionally surface from dives to change our air tanks. It was during the long hours of surface time on another fantastic dive trip, this time to Sulawesi in Indonesia, that I wrote this second edition.

When I am not away diving, I can be found regularly attending and/or speaking at property events. Since the publication of the first edition, I have started a number of associated property businesses, including a training business called TheSourcersApprentice.com which offers training materials for investors – new and experienced. ThePropertySourcers.com also offers a hands-free cashflowing portfolio service to bespoke clients. More about them later...

As I started to write the first edition, I realised that my core principle and driving force is to share knowledge. I guess I will always be a teacher at heart. Therefore, the training business, my second book *Make More Money from Property: From Investor Thinking to a Business Model,* a third book still in development and other training materials are taking that principle still further and into new and different formats.

Above all, I work with cash rich investors to increase the return on their investments by buying and controlling property. I share my expertise and knowledge to enable them to create financial freedom by leveraging the financial resources that they did not necessarily appreciate they had.

I could stop there, but for those of you who know me, I rarely use five words if I can use 50. And for those of you who have heard me speak, you know that I could easily talk about property for five days without taking a breath! So, please allow me to explain how I 'fell' into property investing and show you how easy it can be to use other people's money to build a portfolio that will give you the financial freedom you desire.

My first brush with property came when I was 25 and worked for a mortgage broker. I had always looked at property, noticed it and wondered about it. I loved the job – the organising and the numbers, the talking to people, and helping them to achieve their dreams of owning their own home.

Property kept tapping me on the shoulder and finally I started to listen. In 2001, my sister and I decided to invest in property. This was an important decision, made more challenging because of the journey I had already travelled. To summarise and for completeness, there had been a marriage, two beautiful daughters, isolation, bullying, my ex-husband's bankruptcy, the forced sale of our home just before it could be repossessed (while I was eight months' pregnant with one of my daughters) and then finally a divorce.

As a single mum with two children under three years living on benefits in social housing, I started university and a happier and more empowered life.

It took three years to agree on a property investment strategy. I just knew property was a good idea, but I didn't have any property experience or training. I also learnt that not everyone has the same goals, even though we may use the same words. Words have different meanings and weight for people. This always makes a joint venture a challenge.

My sister and I were lucky. We met a man who turned out to be honourable and very good at his job. We started investing with a pooled pot of money. We later remortgaged and bought more property. It could have so easily been different. I had no experience and no training – no clue in fact, just a feeling… So the journey started and the London portfolio was developed.

Yes, I fell off the wagon. Yes, I have a studio flat in Estonia (anyone want to buy it? It is now very cheap and it might even cashflow!)

Then luck intervened again, I won't rattle on at this point other than to summarise and say that, in 2007, I studied some of the most powerful and mind-expanding courses possible. Since 1993, I had been a university lecturer, completed my first degree and had studied a Master's degree, but I had never heard stuff like this. I learnt that I could control my own mind and my own destiny just by the choices I made and the things I focused on – it was mind blowing! The icing on the cake was to finally understand the power of money, investing and leverage.

Up to now, I had already been doing all of the above, but more by luck rather than design.

Throughout this book, I will be pointing out book titles, people and events that have shaped my life. One of the most profound titles I have read is *The Celestine Prophecy* by James Redfield.

In the story (which is about a man learning to see the world differently) I recognised something of value to me – there are 'messages' (or opportunities if you prefer) all around us, it is our challenge to recognise the important and relevant ones and to act on them. This has never been more important in this social media, information overloaded world. What is important? What will drive you forward towards your goals?

This is an important part of the introduction; in the end, this journey has been borne out of a series of circumstances, of recognising challenges and acting on them. It is this, and the amazing people I have met along the way, which has led me to an incredible career and a dream lifestyle.

Is property the message you have been waiting for? What message is this book holding for you?

Now the hard-core property bit

In 2008, as I finally left the world of personal development, I realised that in seven months of training and crewing I had grown new eyes – in fact a clear and unfogged brain. I started to see things differently.

I finally took notice of a letter that I had already received a number of times before, which invited me to a free two-hour property training event. You would have thought the alarm bells were ringing, but property was the light bulb and I was the moth.

One crucial lesson I have learned over the last three and a half years is that it is vital you know what you want to learn from a training session. Understand the outcomes – are they what you want? If the answer is yes, do the people delivering the course have the current real-world experience you need? When did they last buy a property and what strategy did they use? Finally, how much does the course cost and is it value for money? With so many companies out there, you do not have to pay the £10,000s I paid!

Now put that training into action – start earning back the cost of that educational investment through the knowledge you learnt. I have met so many people who have spent thousands of pounds and yet still have not invested in property or sold a deal. They are still attending courses – actually they are afraid… I have felt like that and I am sure you have too – it's natural.

Why are they afraid? I believe it is either because they are not learning the relevant strategies to help them start, or they do not have the 'right mindset' (dreadful phrase, I know). By this, I mean that they have not aligned their goals and their values in a way that will enable them to take dramatic and unstoppable action – leading to financial freedom.

After my first three days' training, I went out and put everything I knew and understood into practice. By the time we started our next training course some three months later, we were just about to complete on our first property. I was only meant to be practising and I bought a house.

In August 2008, we completed on the 'house from hell'. That's unfair, the house is lovely. However, the vendor was mad, the no money down (NMD) deal was a nightmare, the market volatile, Mortgage Express was just about to close down and rates were rising – a really scary time to start a new career.

It got worse…

From August to November 2008, I didn't manage to buy anything else. House purchases fell through because vendors pulled out, surveyors down valued, there were structural faults, estate agents let me down or I was gazumped.

I lost confidence…

I was networking, but I had no real property friends, mentors or support. I was out of the training loop. I wasn't earning money. I thought I was a professional investor – I had done the training – why wasn't I getting the properties? I even had the 'right mindset'! This wasn't right – something had to change.

What changed?

I made the decision in December 2008 that I was either going to get successful at this or go back to work, and I didn't want to do that – I had a lifestyle mapped out, holidays to take. If I failed, I would make myself get a job at a supermarket stacking shelves – that certainly became a great deterrent.

In January 2009, Bob, my life and business partner, and I took our mentorship as part of that pre-paid training package. The process of going through the theory of investing, demonstrating those skills and receiving feedback certainly helped to repair my confidence. I didn't gain a lot of new knowledge, though sometimes it helps to know that you do know what you think you know!

What this period really confirmed for me was that I was 'trying' to do too many things. Alongside investing in property, I had joined a multi-level marketing (MLM) business. My attention was divided.

From January 2009 onwards, I listened to my coach and I *focused* on what I wanted to achieve, on what I was doing and on what I was learning. Everything was about property and within four weeks I had stopped the other distracting activities and I had another two deals on the table.

I continued to buy, on average, one to two properties a month for the whole of 2009. By the end of 2009, I had a sourcing business doing, effectively, more of the same – buying cashflowing properties for myself and now for fee-paying clients.

Then, in January 2010, I lost focus by writing the first edition of this book! It is easy to know what you should be doing, and often difficult to keep putting the theory into practice, even when you can see it impact on your results! Still, that makes the lesson all the more important and, in a way, proves the point. Focus on One Course Until Successful. As the year progressed, the book became a massive task – not the writing so much as the processes of editing and publishing the book – something I knew nothing about. More distractions…

The following chapters cover everything that I discovered through practice between 2009 and 2012.

They are the techniques needed to buy property today. In the first edition, I asked my property friends, both the famous and the not-so-famous, to share their stories, their tips and recommendations. This time, I am going to focus on supporting friends who are establishing new and vibrant networking groups across the UK – a brilliant way to meet investors and build relationships.

Enjoy reading, listening and watching. Then, if I can ask one thing of you in return, please do something. Do something new or different – just do something with the information you learn here[1].

So why write a book?

I first thought about writing a book in 2008, and I have done a lot of writing for different purposes over the years – as a student for my dissertations, as a lecturer writing academic papers for publication, as a consultant for business, and as part of my personal development training.

I was taught to use writing as a reflective tool and a mechanism to communicate with your own unconscious mind – it is extraordinary the things you can write when you are not consciously thinking about it. Tom Evans – The Bookwright – ran a course that helped me to believe I *could* write a book. In January 2010, I was opening emails that had built up over the Christmas holidays and noticed one from an Ecademy[2] colleague inviting me to contribute to her book *378 Predictions for Doing Business in 2010*.

I immediately recognised this as an opportunity to be part of a product that I could share with others. Then, first thing Tuesday morning, in the shower, I had an even better idea... why not invite all my property friends to contribute their predictions for 2010 and we could produce an ebook together? Even as some people replied, I was already developing the book concept into a bigger project. And so the first edition of *Using Other People's Money: How to invest in property* was borne.

The book concept crystallises

Over the last three years I have spoken at a number of property events and courses. In January 2010 alone, I spoke to over 600 people at various events. The most common question I was asked was: 'I don't have any money, how can I invest in property?'

The answer is, of course, to use other people's money – and that's why I decided to write this book, to share with as many people as possible the

---

1 The videos and audios accompanying this second edition can be obtained through The Sourcers Apprentice website at: http://thesourcersapprentice.com

2 Ecademy.com is an online networking environment that blends the business focus of Linked-In with the social side of Facebook and throws in some events and local meetings for that touch of face-to-face we all love. Email vicki@thepropertymermaid.com if you would like an invitation to join.

knowledge of how to invest in property. This second edition of the book, like the first edition, will help you to recognise how important it is to know how you are going to fund your property investments and to develop those crucial strategies.

What are the crucial finance strategies?

In the 'good old days' all an investor had to do was find a deal and use Mortgage Express to give them a same-day remortgage. They then withdrew all the equity on day one, leaving none of their own cash in the deal. It was that simple to buy a property and literally use none of your own money.

I now believe that led to a lot of bad investment decisions, a lot of laziness. Investors bought 'off-plan' flats that were overvalued by developers and surveyors alike. They over leveraged the properties – taking out high mortgages which left them vulnerable and, for some, over exposed as the prices inevitably started to crumble. Worse, in many cases they didn't even consider how the mortgages would be paid. Yes, by the rent of course, but what about the business basics of supply and demand?

Soon overpriced, over-mortgaged properties in large city-centre blocks were coming up for tenancy renewals and it became a tenant's market place. The result? A dramatic fall in the value of these rents, combined with increasing mortgage rates – a recipe for bankruptcy for many and many months of sheer financial hell. One investor friend was paying £6,000 in mortgages at one point out of his own pocket! Now that is not sustainable investing by anybody's measure.

Sadly, a lot of investors still pursue strategies where their aim is to leave no money in a deal – in effect to be 100% mortgaged. This level of gearing is dangerous in my opinion. We need healthy portfolios with equity in the deal to cover the impact of further house price falls and the inevitable increase in interest rates.

Leaving none of your own money in a deal might sound appealing as you can buy lots of properties, but you will have lots of debt to service too. Why not have fewer properties with a lot of cashflow that covers the cost of borrowing with plenty to spare?

It is more difficult to buy investment properties now. Why is this, if the deals are still relatively easy to find? Principally, because the lenders have realised that they were lending money on property without proper safeguards in place. If the property value fell or the investors could not repay the debt, then there was no cushion to enable the lender to recoup the debt.

Some people say that if the deal is good, then the money will come. I believe that the money comes from the sources you have identified and the strategies you have developed.

This second edition goes one step further in helping you to make money from your property knowledge. It will show you some of the key business principles I have applied over the last two years to grow my business and income even further.

So who is this book for?

Well, *you*. Whether you are new to property investing and not sure how to start when you don't have a bottomless pot of cash to deposit in property, or whether you are an investor experienced in the old ways of working, and maybe even have a highly leveraged portfolio, I believe this book will be useful. New or experienced, I know you will find a gem in this book, a new way of investing or a better understanding of a strategy where you had not previously seen the benefit. Below are just a couple of the hundreds of comments I received about the first edition.

'I saw Vicki talk last night at a property networking event, bought her book and woke up early today to read it. I was so excited – I have properties already, but the money from banks has run out. So I have been struggling with how to get back into the property market with absolutely no money. People I talk to don't believe it can be done, but Vicki is a very ethical person and she knows her stuff. If you have been using the old "I don't have enough money to get into property" excuse, then you now have nowhere to hide as Vicki explains how EVERYONE can get into property. One of the best property books I have read!'

Fiona H

'I've just finished your "manual" on how to raise money. Have put it straight to work and raised £50k from a neighbour who recently sold an inherited house. It also gave me the idea/confidence to ask the divorced owner of a property I am currently buying what he intends on doing with the money! (He had already bought another property.) He came to the conclusion that it would be better to invest his £100k with me. You are right when you say it is a huge responsibility. Thanks for being there.'

Francis D

The environment

The changes in the mortgage markets over the last 3–4 years have caught a lot of people off guard. New investors like me no longer had the luxury of same-day refinancing through Mortgage Express. In fact, even now we are not sure whether a bank will lend, a surveyor will value the property or an offer will last long enough for completion.

That's why we need to get creative, to beat the banks and lenders and not care what rule the Council of Mortgage Lenders dreams up next to protect the banks and finance houses. We need to not care what valuation a surveyor places on a property because we know its true worth – its return on investment (ROI).

In the first edition, I suggested that it is only if you understand the world of money and the history behind it, like the students of Robert Kiyosaki, that you will be able to see the dangers lurking beneath the surface of investment strategies. That, I believe, is the crucial difference – the business acumen that counts – success or failure lies in that sentence.

Instead of seeing the purchase of a property costing very little of your own money as a good idea, for example a £150,000 semi-detached costing just £4,000, a real business entrepreneur (something we need to be in order to be successful in property investing) would understand that you were taking on a £150,000 debt that must be repaid with someone's money – if not the tenants or another buyer's, then *you*! The question to ask is 'What is the net cashflow?'

Let's get educated, professional and creative. Let's invest in property at a time when prices are lower than they have been for years. Let's capitalise on the great cashflows available and let's do it using other people's money wherever possible. However, let's do it using all of our business skills and understanding of the market, our service and of course the power of leverage.

The power team behind the book

I just want to start by acknowledging all the time, support and generosity of the contributors to this second edition. My gratitude goes to the creators of all the new networking groups across England; they are sharing their knowledge, journeys and understanding – you can meet them in the 'Contributors' section of this book on page 149.

There are a couple of other people who I want to acknowledge for their background support. First, Johnnie Cass, my personal coach, for his encouragement to outsource – I finally did it. Second, Andy and Simone Phillips for their advice on internet marketing strategies.

I also have a great business team: Loran Northey who has been my right hand for years and, more recently, has been formally working with me as part of www.ThePropertySourcers.com and www.TheSourcersApprentice.com.

Karin Von Arx, my bookkeeper, and Liam Wall of Bear Space, my accountant and financial director, who are both vital team members!

Having said this, I won't go on and list all of the contributors to the book now, but each one has supported, encouraged or challenged me to be all that I can be – thank you.

I also want to mention my family and friends. I have not seen as much of you over the four years, thank you for being patient with me and for supporting me. It really has been an amazing time. At least when we do meet we have great fun!

And, of course, my dear Bob, who is by no means last. Wow, what has he not done? He's put up with me: first, he let me write the first edition while we were on holiday in South Africa and, this time, I am writing the second edition while on holiday in Sulawesi.

Bob has continued to support me throughout this year of amazing development and opportunity and gives me his endless encouragement, support and belief – thank you, I love you so much.

Everyone needs a 'Bob'. Next year we are planning to make him into an 'App' so everyone can have support whenever they want.

Once again, thank you all so very much.

To our continued wealth, success and beyond…

Vicki Wusche

The Property Mermaid

Chapter 1

In the beginning, there was the mind

This chapter will cover some of the key concepts about how the mind works and how we can train it to work with us in achieving our goals.

How we perceive things – our world model

- Why are some people more successful than others?
- Why are some people happy and others not?

The answers to the above are based on two aspects: first, it is about what you perceive in life. An easy example is the metaphor of 'the glass half full, the glass half empty'. Or getting down to basics, do you even have a glass?

Your success in life is a direct result of the application of two simple skills; focus and gratitude.

Focus

Some people focus only on the bills and their perceived lack of money. Instead of that passive approach, why not take action? Work out your income and expenses, look at bringing your lifestyle and income back into alignment. Make sure you have more money coming in than you have going out. It may seem easy to say, but it's also easy to start doing.

Gratitude

The other skill is to be grateful for what you do have. You are among the 10% richest people in the world by the fact that you live in the western world. A lot of people keep a gratitude journal as a way of reminding themselves, particularly on difficult days, just how much they have to be grateful for. It is easy in our consumer-led, materialistic and fast-paced lives to forget to really appreciate the finer things we have: love, friendship, a home and food to put on the table are just a few.

So what do you 'see' in life?

What you focus on is what you get. Worry about bills and more appear because unconsciously you are looking for them – some would say attracting them into your life (Read *The Secret* by Rhonda Byrne).

The second aspect that determines happiness is who you feel has the power and control in your life. Now, if you are married, you might be tempted to say your partner. The reality is that *we* make decisions and those decisions give us our results. Some people make the decision to give the power and control of their lives to another person. Others struggle, because they have not found the way to reclaim control of their lives.

When I learnt that I had the power to do anything I wanted, and of course with that came the responsibility for the outcome, I was both terrified and liberated. It meant that if I failed, it would be because of the decisions I made. But, equally, if I succeeded, then that would also be as a result of my decisions.

So, if you don't get what you want, how do you think about the situation?

Would you say the house purchase fell through because the lenders pulled out of the deal…? Oh, hold on, this example is not going to work.

What about this example…? If you didn't get a pay rise at work, would the reason be because (1) your boss had it in for you and disliked you, or (2) you had not really been contributing to the team as much as others?

If you answered (1), then it is possible that you see control for your life in the hands of others. If you answered (2), you will recognise that your results, whatever they may be, are directly related to your own actions (or inaction in some cases).

You have the power to change the outcome. This is a much more empowering perspective on life.

I choose to believe that I can do anything I put my mind to. This is a choice, an empowering one. You can choose to believe this too, if you want. Equally, you could choose that nothing ever 'goes your way'.

As a result of this decision, I feel powerful knowing that I can do anything. I also feel proud that I have achieved all that I have because I decided to take action. There was a time when my power was taken from me (notice the language – the power was outside of myself). I was disempowered, isolated and unable to see a way out. I was lost.

I will add one caveat. I totally acknowledge all the support I get. Without Bob at my side my life would be immeasurably harder. I know I can still achieve anything I want to, but it is so much nicer to have company on the journey. Without family, friends and colleagues like Loran Northey (my business partner), Deena Honey, Louise Wheeler and John Cox (partners in my other businesses), my path to success would be longer, harder and much lonelier. Thank you, friends.

What you focus on is what you get

The filters we use to manage the information bombarding our brains and our experiences in life combine to shape how we view the world. You can literally re-programme your brain to think differently.

You must have heard of the saying 'It takes 21 days to create a habit'. It all just takes practice.

Jeff Olson, who wrote *The Slight Edge,* says that success principles start with taking one action every day that is on the path towards your goals. Every day we are faced with choices and, if we make the right choice, we get one step closer to that goal.

You may not realise until years down the line how each simple activity contributed, compounded and grew until success was inevitable. Make the wrong choice and it could be years before you realise the error of your ways and the opportunity you have lost.

Compounding interest and the value of a pound

I have already mentioned the importance of financial intelligence; understanding the power of leverage is crucial. People often ask me how I reconcile being wealthy with the desire to help others. People who work in the social sector find this particularly difficult, as do those whose parents told them 'money was the root of all evil'.

I realised that as I grew my wealth I could in fact contribute more. By investing in buy-to-let properties, I am providing decent homes for people and especially families. As the rent accumulates and I reinvest, I can grow my portfolio and, with that, my ability to support charities and the good works of others.

Have you heard the story that if you take £1 and double it the next day, then double it again the next day, you will have over £1million in 21 days?

Look at the table below. It's 11 days before you get to over £1,000, and 15 days before you get to over £16,000. Then, in the last six days, compounding takes the money to over £1million.

It can be hard to see the benefits of small actions in the early days, one pound at a time, but what about if you know the benefits are multiplying every minute?

Day 1	1	Day 8	128	Day 15	16,384
Day 2	2	Day 9	256	Day 16	32,768
Day 3	4	Day 10	512	Day 17	65,536
Day 4	8	Day 11	1,024	Day 18	131,072
Day 5	16	Day 12	2,048	Day 19	262,144
Day 6	32	Day 13	4,096	Day 20	524,288
Day 7	64	Day 14	8,192	Day 21	1,048,576

Table 1: the powerful effect of compounding

Now compare this table to the second example and table opposite:

What if you took your coffee and applied the same concept? Know that every time you buy a latté or an espresso shot, every time you spend that pound it is lost, it can never be multiplied by you again – it is now multiplying for someone else.

Year	Annum	Lost opportunity
1	-660	660
2	-1,320	1,320
3	-1,980	2,640
4	-2,640	5,280
5	-3,300	10,560
6	-3,960	21,120
7	-4,620	42,240
8	-5,280	84,480
9	-5,940	168,960
10	-6,600	337,920
11	-7,260	675,840
12	-7,920	1,351,680
13	-8,580	Do I need to go on?

Table 2: assume 5 days x £2.75 x 48 weeks = £660.00 per annum

Over 1,351,680 lost opportunities to grow your money from negative compounding – all because you bought a coffee or gave your money away before you made it work for you. Please don't interpret this as being against charitable donations – absolutely we need to give back – but build your capital first and then you can give so much more.

The path to personal development

If there is one thing that we all hear time and time again, it's all about having the 'right mindset'. Some people dismiss personal development and neurolinguistic programming (NLP) as being a bit 'spooky'. Others think they are fine, and a small number embrace the concepts and become really successful.

- Everyone will be successful.
- The question is how successful?

- And how long will it take you to get there?

Get educated – get the learning bug

It doesn't really matter who you listen to, the messages and styles are a variation on a theme. The important thing is to get educated.

Read a personal development book, listen to an audio, go to an event, go to everything free. Expand your understanding of how your mind can work with you or against you. Have that big vision and set those goals, they are so much easier to achieve if you make them real by writing them down. Get a coach if you are serious about being successful. I have two.

Even better, have someone who has done what you want to achieve hold you accountable… That guarantees success!

Understand money and the value of it – this is a critical success factor. We have all heard about the lottery winners who lose everything and more within years of their big wins. Why does this happen? You need to have a wealthy mindset and the right knowledge of how to invest, protect and leverage your money.

Do one thing every day – every day believe in *The Slight Edge*. Do one thing every day towards your goals – one right step.

Manage your mind – the message here is how to work in partnership with your greatest asset. Recognise how much you already have and be grateful, daily. Then plan out your vision, the goals along the way and the actions you need to take on a daily basis to achieve those goals.

As you get your mind on your side, also work on growing your knowledge about wealth, money, how it works and why rich people are rich. Definitely read at least one book by Robert Kiyosaki. I recommend *Conspiracy of the Rich: The 8 New Rules of Money*. This is a comprehensive summary of all Kiyosaki's wisdom to date. Or *The Unfair Advantage*, and then work back through the other books for a deeper understanding.

This brings us neatly to Chapter 2…

Chapter 2

Robert Kiyosaki – the new rules of money

You might wonder when we are going to get to the techniques of using other people's money; how to invest in property. Well, this is all part of it. If you don't know how your mind works (Chapter 1) and you don't know how money works (Chapter 2), then the money you borrow as a result of the techniques discussed later in this book will not create you financial freedom – they may well lead to your financial ruin.

This is neither a game nor a hobby. This is a serious and seriously fun business to be in: exciting and challenging, rewarding and frustrating, but above all wealth creating if you do it right.

In his book, *Conspiracy of the Rich: The 8 New Rules of Money*, Kiyosaki discusses his thoughts on building wealth and how to use other people's money, to buy and build property portfolios.

One of the key things about investing in property or using other people's money is to really understand how money works – to have a high level of 'financial intelligence'. To know the meaning of the terms asset and liability, good debt, bad debt, to understand your financial statement and your level of 'credit-ability' or credibility.

Kiyosaki is very passionate about money and he relays specific messages throughout his books and training to teach people about money. This is something everybody could understand but most people don't think about.

One of his big messages is about ensuring a positive cashflow statement or how we think about money as in terms of assets, expenses and liabilities. In Kiyosaki's eyes, most people treat things incorrectly.

The current dis-education system

It is a real shame we are not taught about money in school or how to use credit properly or what it means. We are all taught to get a job and then buy our home with a mortgage – living happily ever after until the mortgage is paid off in time for us to retire. What the system does not allow for is a low pension, people living longer and being healthier. What do you want your retirement to be like?

I intend to live life to the maximum and I don't want to have to sell my home in order to stay warm and fed. So I choose to do something about it now!

The government has been sending out the wrong message to young people for years, encouraging them to take up student loans and that it's 'OK' to have loans, go to university and end up in massive debt.

All these young people will leave university with £5,000–£20,000 worth of debt. On top of this, when they leave university, they will get a job, meet a partner and, at some point, want to buy a house. However, they will already be saddled with debt before they even consider a mortgage, and with no understanding about how much money it's costing them. Just like we were.

Having said this, if it weren't for 'debt' and the people higher up the money chain making the money from the people lower down the chain through the interest payments, the economy wouldn't be working at all. Our economy is fuelled by debt, by the lending and borrowing of money. The financial sector is one of our major industries.

It is important to understand that there is good debt and bad debt, and everybody should learn the difference. Unfortunately, it's so easy to get bad debt and end up paying four times the ticket price for a seemingly cheap item or paying for the next 20 years.

Good debt vs. bad debt

Good debt is what we use when we invest in property and other 'incoming-generating assets'. An income-generating asset is something that puts money into your pocket even when you don't work.

Good debt is what we use to buy an asset that gives us income in our pockets. We can go on to use the surplus from the rent (money left after the mortgage and house costs are paid) to buy other things, to pay our living costs, so it's using debt in a good way to produce cashflow coming into our pockets.

Bad debt would be something like a loan that you take out to buy a car. You can't earn any money from the car (unless you are a taxi driver). A car immediately loses value, plus there are costs for maintenance. It takes money out of your pocket.

Another example of bad debt is using a credit card to buy a holiday or clothes. If you do not clear the credit card at the end of the month, you will pay interest on the outstanding balance. The interest rates vary, but a holiday for two costing £1,500 at an interest rate of 28% is costing you nearly £35 a month extra.

While the concepts of good debt and bad debt have been explained, it is also important to understand the terms: asset and liability. An asset, like good debt, puts money into your pocket. A liability, by definition, is something that takes money out of your pocket even when you do work.

When we take out a buy-to-let or investment mortgage we are borrowing money from the bank, we are using that debt to buy an asset. We have a tenant who pays for the interest on that debt.

Some people think an example of an asset is the house that they live in, but this is not an asset. As with the example of using a loan to buy a car, your home is not an asset because the mortgage payments are made out of your pocket. The repairs, the bills, the furnishings are all costs to you. Your home is not an asset because it takes money out of your pocket; some people find this explanation and revelation a shock!

Kiyosaki encourages everybody to do research and find a business that will teach them how to sell and speak to people. Lots of property investors and entrepreneurs have second businesses. You need to choose carefully and do your research. Think about where your interests lie – do you want to deal with products or services? In my second book, *Make More Money from Property: From investor thinking to a business mindset,* I recommend that you consider setting up your own property-related business.

I chose to create a property training business because of my background skills as a teacher and my desire to share my knowledge. I also run a property sourcing business, which enables me to focus on sourcing deals and maintaining my contacts and relationships.

Why did I do this? Well, first, because I wanted to enhance and improve my ability to sell, which is a vital skill, and also to build a business and a team. Second, following Kiyosaki's philosophy I wanted to build a business that enabled me to leverage the time of others so I could earn while I was not working.

Property enables me to leverage my money and business enables me to leverage my time and that of my team/business partners.

This business is all about selling, life is all about selling: what to have for dinner, where to go out, who to date, what property to buy or sell, what business to invest in.

I have had multi-level marketing (MLM) businesses (two in fact) and I found that they distracted me as they were not about property – I believe focus is crucial. So, if you know how to do something, why not monetise that activity?

Cashflow – Monopoly on steroids

In order to help you understand more about money and how it works, Kiyosaki and his wife, Kim, created their Cashflow board game – Kiyosaki refers to it as 'Monopoly on steroids'. The game is played in groups at organised Cashflow Clubs across the UK, which are designed to teach and help you to play the game with others.

Kiyosaki talks a lot about the 'cone of learning'. If you practise what you're learning, you retain the information better. If you don't live in London, then a good place to find your nearest official Cashflow Club is at: www.meetup.com/.

Use the search tool and bring up all the Cashflow Clubs in the UK. At an official club, you'll go along, listen to a recorded talk by Kiyosaki, participate in a discussion about the current learning topic and, after the discussion, you will play the game amongst other people. You will learn different techniques, see how others manage their money and think about what you do and about how you treat money.

After the game there is a debrief session and you'll discuss what happened in the game. Kiyosaki recommends that you play the game 10 times, because each time you play the game you will learn a different lesson.

It is essentially a board game, where you are given pieces of information and have to make decisions. These decisions have consequences and at the end of the game you can reflect back on the consequences and the results of the decisions you made, and learn how to make better decisions.

Your financial statement – what is it and what does it mean?

It is definitely *not* about your bank statement and how much money you put into the bank or take out. A financial statement shows your assets, your liabilities, your income and expenses. Once you have mapped out all of this, you can see the state of your finances – in a sense your financial position. Some people may have bought assets that don't actually cashflow, or they may have a negative cashflow across the whole portfolio that could be solved by selling just one property.

Over-reliance on the State

Kiyosaki is passionately against the general public's over reliance on the 'State' for money, whether it is pensions, sick pay or unemployment benefit – even our health care is government funded. In his book, *Conspiracy of the Rich: The 8 New Rules of Money*, Kiyosaki explains how the government cannot afford to pay all the money it owes in promised future pensions. To rely on the government for your forthcoming old age is not a good plan.

However, if you build up your own assets and those assets put money in your pocket, then you will be self-sufficient when you are older. You can still collect your pension if there is one, but you won't be reliant on it. That is my plan!

Unfortunately, with the devaluation of money in real terms, your savings won't buy you much in 20 years. However, income-generating assets will increase in value and rise in line with inflation. When you understand how the money flows and the real value of the assets that you own, then you will be in a strong position for the future.

Are you living above your means? You really need to understand your financial position if you are going to be really financially successful.

History of money and why it's not worth anything now

Historically, the way money is viewed, used and valued has changed dramatically. It was switched from the 'Gold Standard' back in 1971 and now it's almost become valueless.

Until the 1970s, the US dollar was pegged against gold. In other words, you could exchange your dollar for gold. This system was removed in the 1970s and now money is simply a debt note. These debt notes can be bundled together and sold as a product. These derivatives enabled the banks to sell bundles of bad debt as a product with a value. It's madness and almost incomprehensible.

It also means that a government can now print money when it decides, because it does not need the gold to back up that debt note. We have already seen the British government print extra money as part of the quantitative easing program. If there are more pound notes in circulation, then the value of each note effectively decreases and inflation becomes a real danger.

When you compare things like stocks and shares to gold, they are actually reducing in value; if you compare property to gold, it has maintained its value level. Kiyosaki is very vocal in his belief that, in relative value terms, a dollar means nothing any more, it's just a piece of paper that is backed by nothing. He feels this is a dangerous position for any country to place itself in.

Controlling assets – taking the first step

You have far more control over an asset than you have over money in the bank. With an asset like property, you can buy it at a discount and add value by renovating or adding rooms.

You can manage your income by managing your tenant, who ultimately provides the cash through rental payments. In reality, your tenant is also your asset, not just the bricks and mortar.

The property investment journey starts with understanding and getting educated first. Do things the right way; don't expose yourself to any uncalculated risks by not having the right information.

- Start slowly and it won't be long before you never look back.
- And, of course, beware of the sharks swimming in the property investment pool.
- Take those first small steps and change things.
- Don't ever just take one person's word; listen to a number of people.

As I mentioned before, Jeff Olson, the author of the book *The Slight Edge*, states that every day we have the choice to make the right decision and, if we make that right decision day after day, it's not long before the benefits of our decisions and actions create exponential growth.

Chapter 3

Buying with credit cards – tread carefully

Understanding how to use credit cards (or any form of bank lending) to your own advantage is vital if you are to make the best use of your investment capital and cashflow. Credit cards and the companies that run them are notorious for charging high rates of interest on any outstanding balances. Many of you will already have credit cards and use them regularly.

A surprising number of you will still hold the old view that credit cards are 'bad'. In this chapter, the aim is to explain how you can use credit cards to your advantage, avoid high interest charges and pitfalls, and increase your investment capital.

I thought you said credit cards were bad?

Let's start with dispelling the myth that credit cards are bad news. What makes them 'good' or 'bad' is how you use them. For example, going on a 'shopping spree', whether it's clothes, electronics or holidays, and not clearing the outstanding balance on your statement in full is not only bad it is mad. To explain briefly, this is because the outstanding balance will accrue interest at the high rate that your card company charges, often in excess of 29%. Therefore, any savings made at the point of purchase is not only wiped out but actually exceeded by the ongoing monthly costs charged by the company. I will come to some more examples later on.

So, if you use credit cards to buy frivolous items or 'stuff' that does not ultimately return an income, then, yes, they are bad news. Credit cards teach you to spend what you don't have without thought for clearing the debt. However, in its simplest form, a credit card, if used properly, can give you up to 45 days extra money – interest free.

Let me just explain that last sentence. Immediately after you receive your last credit card statement and demand for payment, you could buy products or services using the 'credit' available on your credit card. Then you would have use of that money/credit for approximately 45 days or longer until your next credit card statement and demand for payment arrives in the post.

This is using a credit card for maximum gain, your gain. By buying products like building materials or paying for surveys on your credit card, you can effectively keep your actual cash in your bank account for a further 45 days.

I guess some of you are already thinking about skipping this chapter – please don't. This section will discuss some of the facts, tips and information 'not widely' known about credit cards, credit rating and how to protect your score while getting the maximum possible out of the banks.

What the bank wants

Banks want you to stay ignorant of the game and how it works. They want you to take out credit cards and buy stuff that really you can't afford, so that at the end of the month you don't clear your credit card balance and instead pay them an extortionate rate of interest.

On the other hand, they now also want you to be the model and perfect borrower. From a secured lending perspective, the underwriters of mortgages want you to demonstrate that you know how to manage your money. The way that you do this is to limit the amount of unsecured borrowing (credit cards) that you have available. Do not apply for too many credit cards and do not 'max out' your credit cards, using every last pound available to you, as you will look out of control. And, of course, pay back your cards regularly and even overpay them now and then. Let's take all of these points in turn and turn the tables on the banks and lenders.

Limit the number of cards that you have

Let's start with the situation that you already have six or more credit cards. At this point, I would suggest that you review all of your cards, how you use them, how you clear the balances and, of course, check your credit rating. If you have a good score, and we discuss this in more detail on page 19, then leave things alone.

Alternatively, if you have a lot of cards and a poor score, it could imply that you are not managing your cards well – we discuss some good habits for managing your cards on page 18.

You may be one of a surprisingly large number of people that either do not have a credit card or have only one or two in their name. This is perfectly fine and please do not rush out and apply for another six cards! The same principles apply to you as everyone else. Think about how you currently use your cards and how you clear them.

Check your credit rating and if you have a very good score and you are not just about to apply for a mortgage, then you might want to consider applying for a new credit card – especially if there is a 0% offer available. However, there is no point getting a 0% offer if you do not have a specific business reason and use for the money.

Do not apply for too many

I just mentioned applying for a new card and now I am saying don't apply for too many. Of course you can apply for a new credit card, but I would suggest that you have a specific reason or use for applying for it. Only apply for a credit card if you have checked that your credit report and credit score are in good order. And definitely, in my opinion, do not apply for a credit card just before you want to apply for a mortgage, as the credit card company will conduct a credit search on you and this will be recorded on your credit report. It may not count against you, but do you want to take the risk? Think about your actions and plan carefully.

It is good practice to have one or two cards that you use to purchase goods (shopping or petrol) on a regular basis, and then pay them off in full every month. You might also have one or two cards that you use for 'business' purposes, such as paying surveyor or broker fees. Again, clearing the card monthly.

You may also have borrowed money on a 0% credit card to fund the cost of materials for a refurbishment project, like a new kitchen or plumbing materials, then you would be making only minimum payments. Imagine looking at your credit report through the eyes of an underwriter who is considering lending you a lot of money on a mortgage. This sort of behaviour might look like someone who knew how to manage their finances.

Alternatively, if as an underwriter you saw a credit report that had a number of applications for credit cards one month and then more the next month, you might consider that this person was desperate to get hold of credit and that they may be out of control or a high risk.

Don't 'max out' your credit limit

This is very similar in principle to the point about the number of cards you have. Credit reports record the activity on your credit card – this is explained further on page 20. Imagine you are an underwriter considering whether or not to approve a loan. Which person would you think was a better risk: the person who had a number of cards all with maximum borrowing that were not cleared monthly, or the person who had a number of cards, some cleared in full and others with a modest outstanding balance?

It is good practice to make sure that you do not over use every last bit of credit available on your card, while at the same time making sure that you use up to the limit and clear it regularly. This may sound confusing but think of it this way: be very aware of your credit limit and on certain cards work carefully to spend close to your limit by the end of the monthly period and then clear down the balance. This way you are showing the card lender that you need that amount of credit limit and you can manage your financial affairs carefully. However do not use all your cards to the very limit all the time without clearing them regularly as, again, you may look desperate for cash.

Pay back regularly and even overpay

It is absolutely vital that you set up a direct debit on all cards and, in fact, all loans that you take out. Make sure that you know exactly how much available cash you need in your bank account to pay the minimum payments. By using direct debits you avoid the fatal error of missing a payment. Missed payments are, in the eyes of underwriters, the sign of a careless borrower or someone whose borrowing is out of control. Your credit score will be affected and most mortgage lenders will refuse to lend to you if you demonstrate this behaviour.

It can be good practice to occasionally overpay on your cards. If you have a 0% card offer, then set up a direct debit and each month make an extra payment to show that you can afford to clear the debt. If you are using a card for regular monthly expenses, then each month you will know that the amount outstanding on the card, and due for payment, is actually more in real terms as you will have continued to spend. So make the occasional overpayment. If the statement states that you owe £500 and you know in real terms it is closer to £600, then pay more than the £500 to show that you can.

How can you use credit cards to your advantage?

Credit cards, if used properly, can fund the refurbishment of properties, as mentioned above, or fund the deposits to buy new properties. They are simply another means of getting money for nothing, or very cheaply if you do it right.

They are a relatively easy and, of course, unsecured way to access additional money. However, like all things involving money, interest payments and time limits, they only work if you know what you are doing. Let's get into the detail and discuss credit scores.

The do's and don'ts of credit cards and your credit score

Your credit score needs to be managed carefully.[3] Contact the credit reference agencies like Equifax and Experian and look at your credit score. You should be aiming for an Experian credit score of 999. Make sure that all the information they hold about you is correct and rectify any information that is incorrect or missing, so that your credit record is accurate. You might ask, why contact both agencies? This is because different lenders use different companies, and the companies themselves hold slightly different information on you. Experian – used by the likes of HBOS[4] group and Birmingham Midshires – hold approximately one year of detailed information on you. So, as long as you do not miss payments or over apply for cards, you will likely have a good score.

Let's just re-emphasise the following two statements, as I believe they are the foundation to using your credit cards expertly:

- Do not miss a payment – it is vital that every single credit card that you have is set up with a minimum direct debit in place. If anything happens, such as a postal strike or holiday, then you know your payments will always be made.
- Don't over apply for cards – there is a temptation to apply for lots of cards once you learn the system. Don't! It will significantly reduce your credit score. Why? Because one of the 'markers' or factors that lenders look at is how many loan or credit applications you have made.

---

3   Credit scores are a system used by credit rating agencies to give you a numerical value based on the risk you pose to lenders. The higher the score (top score 999), the better potential client you are. The lower the score, the worse risk you present to a lender. The risk is whether you will default on your payments.

4   HBOS – Halifax, Bank of Scotland – a bank and mortgage lender.

Experian obtain information about your card applications in two ways: one from the number of searches on your record; and two from the number of applications that actually hit your record. Every time you apply for a credit card there will be a search. Searches can take between one and three months to show on your credit file, depending on how quickly the company you applied to acts.

Too many searches will reduce your credit score. Future lenders will be able to see these searches and lenders do not like to see too many, as this may make you look as though you are desperate for money and will make them cautious about lending. This time delay between applications and the information hitting your credit file often catches people out, especially when applying for mortgages, as mortgage lenders like to see a high credit rating and low searches listing.

Let's talk about Equifax and how they are different from Experian. Equifax keep records of your payments for over 10 years. What does this mean? Well, if you have been less reliable with your money in the past, missing payments, etc., then this will show on your record. It also shows your month-by-month credit limit, statement amount and payment amount. Lenders viewing an Equifax report can see how much you pay each month.

Why is it so important to understand about credit reports and how the companies work? Well, lenders have to lend a certain amount of money each month (they have budget or target figures). Once they reach this target (or get close to it), they will start to get choosier about who they lend money to and will raise the minimum credit score limit. So, in the first few weeks of a month (and again on a quarterly basis), lenders may offer mortgages to people with scores as low as 800 (a good rating normally), but then suddenly anything less that 995 (which is excellent and only 4 points away from perfect) would be rejected as not good enough.

Also, you may have no problem getting loans from Birmingham Midshires (BMS), and then suddenly be refused by The Mortgage Works (TMW) because they use Equifax. As more mortgage products start to come to the market, it is highly likely that they will only offer the more advantageous products to the better clients with the best credit reports and scores – and you want that to be you.

| VERY POOR | POOR | FAIR | GOOD | EXCELLENT |

How do banks score?

Your own bank will score you differently as it can see what you spend on a daily basis. The bank understands how your money goes in and out of your account. Of course, the bank likes to see that you are paying in more money than you are withdrawing on a monthly basis. They have a more intimate knowledge of you, especially if you have been a client for years and have a number of accounts. Alternatively, you may find your high street bank is not offering products that are favourable to you as a prospective property investor. You will need to discuss commercial lending on a business basis and that is another whole chapter in its own right.

What if I have a bad score?

If you don't have a good credit score, you can pair yourself with someone who does, but you need to bear in mind that you are entwining yourself in a business relationship and consider whether this is something you really want to do. It is important to consider that the person with the good score may not want to be 'financially associated' with you, as this link will remain on their credit score indefinitely.

A better approach is to set up a joint venture where the person with the good credit score takes responsibility for the mortgage and you with the poor score do all the work to find and manage the property, and then you agree a form of profit share. This way you are not 'financially' linked as far as your credit reports are concerned. However, if your husband, wife or partner has a good score, then simply by living in the same house you are linked financially, so there is no advantage or disadvantage to applying for a joint mortgage from a credit report perspective.

Some credit cards are the same but in disguise

When applying for cards it is important that you are aware of what company owns which credit card brand. It is important to pick different companies as a credit card lender will only want to lend you a certain amount of money.

As a professional property investor, you will have some idea about what mortgage companies want (or at least as much of an idea as any of us at the moment). Now you understand how to work the credit card companies, knowing the interest rate on the card and the balance transfer rate is essential. Even when transferring over to a 0% card, there will still be some charges. Also, the credit card company will never lend you the full amount of your available balance because they want to keep a reserve on your account, to cover interest charges and any purchase you might make.

What is gearing?

Gearing is when a lender looks at how much you have actually borrowed, particularly on unsecured lending like credit cards, against how much available credit you have. You need to get to a position where you are borrowing under 60% of your potential borrowing – i.e. have a gearing ratio of less than 60%. How do you work this out? Add up the total debt on all your credit cards and divide it by the total of all your credit limits.

It may take a while, but gradually reduce any outstanding balances by overpaying – particularly any card that is accruing interest. Then, once in a while, maybe every other month, apply for a new credit card. If it is a 0% balance transfer card, then transfer and clear existing balances where you are paying interest charges. Your aim should be to reduce your total borrowing and eradicate any borrowing where you pay interest, except for example mortgages because in fact your tenant pays for that anyway.

Top tip

You can get some credit cards that transfer an outstanding credit balance direct into your bank account – check out MBNA and their associated cards (Egg used to do this but they have been bought by Barclays and we've yet to see if the practice will continue). The end goal is to get any outstanding balance you have on a card transferred into your bank account.

These funds can then be used as cash or funds for a refurbishment, a deposit for a house purchase or maybe an outright purchase. For example, use £20,000 towards the deposit and know that you are going to sell within a year and clear the card before the end of the 0% period. This is an excellent way to use credit cards for your own purpose and not get sucked into the whirlpool of debt that banks need us to be in.

Summary – good habits for managing your credit cards effectively

- Obtain your credit reports and credit scores regularly – at least every other month and check the information.
- Minimise the number of applications you make to a maximum of one a month and fewer than three in six months (even that could be high now). Also know which companies are affiliated, such as Virgin and MBNA. Do not reapply if you have just been turned down – wait until you get your credit reports, repair the problem and then wait again before continuing.
- ALWAYS set up a direct debit payment and then overpay each month as you see fit.
- Keep a spreadsheet and track each card: know your credit limit, know when you last asked for an increase, know when your 0% deal runs out and clear that card first.
- Aim to bring your gearing ratio down by making focused payments.
- Clear any cards that are accruing interest charges as a priority.
- Remember, good debt is for purchases that earn you money, for example a property purchase or refurbishment, and bad debt is the purchase of goods or services that reduce in value and cost you money.
- Finally, whatever you are going to invest in when using your credit card, you must know how you will get the money back to repay your cards.

How it works in practice

When I was in my poor phase as a single mother, literally counting every single 10 pence piece I spent, the credit card was my saviour. I put my money in a high-rate deposit account, spent everything I could on my credit card. Wait, let me rephrase that… I made every payment I could by credit card – while still knowing my budget and my income. I then cleared the credit card every month in full from the savings account – one withdrawal.

At the end of the year, the bank gave me between £60 and £100 interest for managing my money – which the girls and I spent on our summer holidays and having fun. It might not seem like a lot, but it was a great return for relatively little effort, in a time when my budget for food and entertainment was very limited!

Since early 2000, I have played the 0% off-set game. To do this, you need an 'Off-set' or 'One' mortgage account (at the time of writing Barclays, Woolwich, Virgin and even Halifax are offering them). Essentially, all your money is totalled up every month and the total debt (your mortgage) and your total savings (wages, account balance, etc.) counteract one another.

For example, if you have a £100,000 mortgage and £5,000 joint income, then at that point you only owe £95,000. The next day, after a few bills, you may have £4,500 in your account, so now you owe £95,500 and that is the figure you pay mortgage interest on. However, you don't earn interest on your savings. It's brilliant in today's market where you are better off off-setting your mortgage, as mortgage interest is 3–6% and savings interest only 1–2%.

Now I have all my cards on direct debit minimum payments and then I regularly overpay each account. So, if I have £10,000 on a 0% card and a minimum payment of £25 each month, then when the bill comes in I will also make an online payment of between £20–£100 extra. Why? To show the lenders I am capable of paying back more than the minimum.

In early 2010, I built up a credit limit of over £20,000 on one of my cards through the MBNA group. I then applied for a 0% balance transfer and got that money transferred into my bank account where I then used it to buy a property.

The pitfalls

Using credit cards is potentially a risky strategy if you do not know how to use them properly. However, throughout this chapter I have explained and shown examples of how you can monitor and improve your credit rating, borrow money from credit cards often at 0% and extend the use of your own personal cash reserves, plus a whole range of techniques to protect you and your credit rating. Now, before you actually start using credit cards to invest in property, you need to clearly understand your actual investment strategy and how you are going to pay back this loan.

The money borrowed from a credit card, if done well, is a loan at 0% for a limited period of time. You must have in place one, if not two, strategies to clear that debt in full before the end of the term, otherwise you will be paying close to 29% in interest. This strategy must only be used where you know that you can remortgage a renovated property or that you can sell or remortgage a buy-to-let property and release funds to clear the debt.

Credit cards are a brilliant way to extend money and, if they are used correctly, they can increase your credit profile, which enables more lending. If used properly, they are a superb resource of quick and often very cheap funds that can enhance your personal cashflow, making deals more manageable and ultimately more profitable. Remember, always plan what you intend to spend the money on and know how you are going to release the funds back out to repay the borrowing.

Chapter 4

Working with banks – boutique and commercial lending

This chapter explains a little about commercial lending. I first approached the high street banks in 2009 to see whether I could borrow money to invest in property. This meant having conversations as a business client of the bank, which entails a whole different language. I am briefly going to explain what (little) I know about the money markets, (even less) how the banks work and how I have used commercial bank lending to invest in property (it's mind blowing).

A brief history – banking and the money markets

During 2008 and 2009, the availability of money in the marketplace and high street was severely constricted as banks and mortgage lenders pulled out of the lending market either through poor performance or simply the lack of trust and resultant short supply of funds available to lend. This has continued to be the case during 2010 and 2011, and certainly the early part of 2012.

It is my opinion that, while some practices will gradually creep back into the lending market, such as 85% lending, there will be a new sense of caution and restriction for many years to come. This is not only because the banks got burnt, they are actually in an incredibly vulnerable financial position. They are unbalanced, which is why we have seen moves by some high street banks to recapitalise their balance sheets by calling in business overdrafts and even loans!

I am not going to cover the whole history of banking, just a brief summary of key points as a way to set the scene from the banks' perspective. It is important to understand where the money you eventually borrow from a bank originated from. In the old days, as people worked and accumulated surplus cash, they deposited it in the bank for safekeeping. This money was lent to other people for a fee.

While there is still a business based around lending money that a bank (or building society) has received as deposits from savers, money is now also 'bought' and traded on the money markets. This has become a major industry in its own right across the world.

The money, in some senses, still comes from 'people' who have surplus cash, just on a massive and inconceivable scale. You may have heard the comment that trillions and trillions of pounds are circulating around the globe at any one time. Also remember that since the separation from the Gold Standard, it is in fact all just paper and debt!

The banks 'buy' money for a fee. The average interest rate calculated on a daily basis is called the LIBOR (London InterBank Offered Rate).This is best explained as the interest rate that banks pay for the money they borrow. They can choose to borrow money for set periods and LIBOR has rates for three or six months, and one or more years. Though this may all change following recent scandals.

It is quite interesting to look at these rates and see how they change over time. Analysts use this information as a measure of the confidence in the market. The higher the rate, the lower the confidence and the greater the pressure to increase the Bank of England base rate.

There are hundreds of banks

If you ask Google how many banks there are in the world, the answer is over a million. On the one hand, this is encouraging because if one turns you down, then you can simply approach another. It can also seem overwhelming: the challenge of how to approach banks, which ones to pick and what to say.

There is another question: why would you want to use a commercial or boutique bank as your lender? The best reason is because they will consider you as a complete person or business, unlike mortgage lenders who see you as a credit score and a specific property. They also 'create' or offer you a lending product that is bespoke to the risk that you present. This means that the more successful they consider you and the lower risk you present, then the more preferential the terms of the loan. I cover this a little later on page 30.

When approaching these business-orientated banks, you will need to present yourself differently – you will need to prepare. The banks are going to want to get to know you on an individual basis and to meet you face to face. They will want details of your existing business and investments, details of your income, expenditure, assets and liabilities (hence the inclusion of Chapter 2).

They are, of course, going to consider your credit history, which may be good but because of lots of credit cards or mortgage applications may be tied to a lower score. This will not go against you to the degree it does when applying to an ordinary 'production-line' mortgage lender.

If this sounds daunting, one approach is to speak to your broker and explain that you want to approach a commercial or boutique bank. They will be able to help and advise you. If not, do it yourself. You have nothing to lose and everything to gain.

Commercial lending or a mortgage – What's the difference? What's the point?

In some ways there is no difference and I will explain why in a minute. Where there is a difference, it is in the philosophy or culture of the organisations that are lending you the money, and that's very noticeable. The banks are old and, in some senses, old-fashioned institutions. They are a contradiction of highly cautious and, yet, extraordinary risk taking.

When you start a conversation with a bank about commercial lending, they will want to follow a very similar process to a mortgage lender. First, the banks will want to know that you are a safe business for the money they are going to lend you. So they will check your credit score, but, more importantly, they will want to meet you face to face (initially) to understand your business model – how it works, where you make money and why it is a good idea.

I talk later in the book (Chapter 6) about creating your own investor pack or private finance document, where you explain your experience and justify your strategy. This is exactly the sort of information the bank is looking for. So in a sense they are going to credit score you, but also investigate your business model and your experience. As you can imagine, this is much more in depth and initially time consuming than applying for a decision in principle (DIP), but, for some of you, well worth being considered as a whole entity.

Second, the banks will want to know that they can obtain security for the money they are going to lend you. They will take, in principle, anything of a similar value. This means it does not have to be the actual house you are buying. It could be another unencumbered property, shares, cash savings or, if you are in that market, even gold deposits can be used as collateral. In its simplest form, they will carry out a survey on the investment property.

Now the bank will discuss terms for the lending. These are negotiable! Which means, within reason, the better business proposition you are and the less risk you present, the more preferential the agreed rates.

There are several components to a commercial loan:

1. **The exposure or loan to value** – In simple terms, how much the bank is prepared to lend you against the collateral you are offering. At the moment, they are mostly offering a maximum of 70%. However, you might be able to find higher.

2. **The cost of the money or the interest rate** – Now it is important to be careful here, because most commercial lending is on a capital and repayment basis, not interest-only as with buy-to-let mortgages. Banks use phrases like 'pay rate', which means they will offer you a pay rate of 3.5%, for example, over the base rate (which is currently 0.5%), giving a total loan rate of 4% capital and repayment. (This will feel like a rate of 7%+ if it is an interest-only equivalent loan.)

3. **Coverage** – This means that you must have sufficient income (rent) to cover the cost of repaying the debt. Banks express this as a percentage. In a normal mortgage, they look for 125% coverage. All banks will be different but, essentially, they do not count the full annual rent as income, they assume a percentage of void and maintenance costs. So they may only consider 70% of rental income and then expect that to cover the loan cost by a rate of 140%, for example. You will need to really understand this part of your agreement, otherwise you may find that none of your deals will actually be acceptable.

4. **Finally, there is the term of the loan** – Just as with normal mortgages, this will be based on age. However, because the bank assumes that you will keep the loan and clear it in full through monthly payments (capital and repayment), then this can make your monthly payments quite high and, in turn, affect your ability to provide rental cover. They will refer to the 'amortization' of the loan – how the capital portion of your mortgage reduces the actual debt.

This does sound complicated but is in fact really easy to understand, when once again you put yourself in the position of the lender. They want to lend money safely, knowing that you can afford to repay the debt, and, if not, that they have sufficient security to recoup their money if need be. After all, they have most likely paid to borrow the money on the open market in the first place.

Why is commercial lending a good idea?

Before I explain how I use this type of lending, let me just explain a handful of great reasons to borrow from a bank.

1. **Much cheaper fees**. Unlike mortgage companies, banks do not charge 2–3.5% admin fees – fees can be just a few hundred pounds. However, the surveys can cost about £500 instead of £300.

2. **Banks do not operate a 'six-month rule' on commercial lending**. So they do not care if the previous owner only bought the property three months ago.

3. **Banks do not charge 'early redemption charges' (ERC)**. Therefore, although there is a term (length) to the loan, you are not tied into that lending product like you are with a buy-to-let mortgage.

Now look at points 2 and 3 above together. You can buy any property you like (providing it meets the lending criteria), and then either resell it on the open market or remortgage it after refurbishment at closer to its full market value.

You can achieve this with some building society lenders now. Check with your broker to see what is current in the market.

One last thing you should know

Again, it is about banking language and culture. You will need to 'find' a business manager who deals with commercial lending. That sounds a little odd, but not every branch has a commercial function; a lot of high street branches are for the general public use only.

Once you find a branch that has a commercial department, and of course you are fully prepared with your investor pack, you will want to ask for an appointment with someone with appropriate experience. You want to make an appointment with a business manager or relationship manager, or sometimes a portfolio manager who works with property investors.

Why? Because your business is not like a normal retail business. In most cases, you will be looking for the bank to lend you money for trading purposes. You will be buying and either selling or remortgaging property through them. So large amounts of debt will be cleared often within 12 months and then re-borrowed. This is not normal practice and so you need someone who has experience.

How did I use commercial funding?

In early 2009, I started to approach high street banks. Initially, I took the attitude (to help build my confidence) that I was interviewing them to see which bank could offer me the best service and help my business grow. From the outset, I was well prepared with a presentation and my investor pack. As I progressed to my third 'interview', I learnt through listening to their questions what interested the bank most, and then focused on supplying only that information and the answers to their questions.

Initially I opened an account with an experienced branch manager, but soon realised that I needed more immediate service. Branch managers often look after upwards of 250 businesses. I eventually met and transferred my business to a relationship manager in London. The service operation was completely different. He worked with a maximum of 50 businesses and had his own dedicated administrator. He also worked with businesses that turned over in excess of £1million per annum. It was a totally different type of relationship all together.

Once I had established this relationship I could use commercial funding to buy a property for effectively no money down with their full knowledge and understanding. How? I would ask the bank for a remortgage on a property that I currently did not own but that I actually intended to buy. Let me break that down. I would find a suitably undervalued property, make my offer to the vendor and get it accepted in the normal way. I would then apply for a remortgage rather than a mortgage from the bank.

The bank would carry out a credit check, instruct the survey and eventually make the official offer in the normal way. However, the surveyor would be examining the property with the remortgage value in mind. I never told him the purchase price because I was not buying, I was remortgaging.

Once I had the offer for the remortgage in my hands, I would go ahead and buy the property for cash at the under market value. Within a week, my solicitor would then carry out the remortgage.

Two minor points: we waited a week so that the solicitor could process all the sale papers and then properly remortgage the property; I used my off-set mortgage mentioned at the end of Chapter 3 on page 24 to temporarily fund the purchase.

This was all legal and with the bank's knowledge. They knew I would have only owned the property for under a month – they did not have a six-month rule so this did not matter. I used the bank's survey and the bank's remortgage offer as my personal security checks before I bought. I never bought without having an offer in place to enable me to pull my money back out and repay my off-set mortgage.

Some properties were effectively no money down and others even gave cashback to cover the cost of the remortgage and buying process.

After six to nine months, I would recheck the lending rates in the market and the current values of the property and remortgage a second time. This time the property was remortgaged to a lender because the rate was good and the loan on an interest-only basis. This does not always result in that much more cash from the property in terms of money released, but it does dramatically improve the cashflow.

The sting in the tail

The door closed on this approach of remortgaging at full market value last year. However, commercial lending is still a great way to buy a property without paying early redemption charges or being liable to the six-month rule. This lending is perfect for refurbishing and flipping small properties quickly without incurring penalties.

During 2012, I continue to seek out commercial banks that are open-minded to building relationships with property investors and business owners. I would recommend that investors based inside the M25 – buying local properties – check out MetroBank. They are a new London-based bank that is set on doing business differently – at the very least they offer business accounts that are charge free! Depending on their mood, Lloyds Bank has also been very interested in commercial lending.

It is different

This is a different way of borrowing money and, like with credit cards, you need to understand what the lender wants to achieve and what they want from you.

- Are you the owner of a sound business, well justified with appropriate experience?

- Can you provide appropriate levels of collateral, either through the investment property or other ways?
- Can you afford to pay back the loan, through the rent on the property and maybe through a partner's employed income?
- What does the internet say about your business, the bank will check your website?

Ultimately, the lender wants to know whether you are going to be a good customer from whom they can make money.

Certainly in my case, banks really liked the fact that Bob was employed and had a regular income – this provided additional security and peace of mind.

They obviously wanted us to transfer our business account to them. They were happy that we (temporarily) deposited a fair sized cash lump sum in the account (which we later drew out over a couple of months and paid back to our off-set mortgage).

Think like a professional investor, present yourself as a serious and knowledgeable business owner, show the bank that you know what you are talking about and have a track record of success, or that you are planning to have a track record of success.

Chapter 5

No money down deals – or mortgage fraud, you decide!

What is a no money down (NMD) deal?

The principle of a NMD deal is that you do not leave any of your own money in the deal. This is different from recycling your cash, in that the money never really goes into the deal at the start. During 2009 and 2010, when lending rules changed and the strategy of same-day remortgaging was 'outlawed' by lenders, a large number of property sourcers and deal packagers identified a flaw in the lending rules.

They used specific systems and a couple of solicitors to effectively manipulate the lenders into fully funding a property purchase. What I mean by this is that the purchase of the property is fully funded by a loan. OK, so what if part of the loan was from the bank and the other part from a family member, credit card or angel investor? Would that be a NMD deal? Yes, I agree that it would, but I use the phrase 'using other people's money' to make the distinction.

In the capital letter sense of NMD, and in 2010 and 2011 the second term 'below market value' (BMV), what some providers or companies were suggesting was a 'particular and specific system' that resulted in the mortgage lender funding the full 100% of the mortgage. Now we all know that they definitely don't want to do that. So these schemes used a variety of tactics to elevate the purchase price of the investment property, for example by using irrevocable agreements, fees or sub-sales. I am not going to explain the tactics in detail, other than to say the one thing they nearly all have in common is the need to use at least two solicitors on the buyer's side.

The other thing the schemes have in common is the risk of being accused of mortgage fraud, over gearing a portfolio and lower cashflow. The result is that many investors have built portfolios using these systems that are now 100% mortgaged with low cashflow! In my opinion, that is not the foundations of financial freedom.

To show the distinction – if you buy a property and refurbish it and in that process genuinely increase the value so that at remortgage you can pull your costs out, then that is brilliant. In fact, you will have a cashflowing portfolio (providing you get the sums right) that is still only geared (borrowing) 75% of the value – you will still have a genuine 25% equity.

Great minds think alike

You will notice that I feel very strongly about these systems. I would have loved to find a NMD system that I was comfortable with. Part of my problem is that I want to understand the contracts and deals that I am getting into, and when a deal maker or sourcing agent won't or can't explain the finance system to me, then I feel uncomfortable. My comfort (moral) line in the ground may well be in a different place to yours.

Above all, I would like people reading this book to be more aware of the financial system they are using and enter into contracts with their eyes fully open, then decide whether they feel comfortable or not. You need to understand the difference between owning a lot of properties and owning a cashflowing portfolio which generates enough cashflow to meet your monthly expenses and means you are financially free! A lot of properties do not guarantee financial freedom, a lot of cashflow (profit) does!

In some ways, all of the strategies in this book are NMD deals. Why? Because they all suggest ways that you can use other people's money to invest in property. Another way to think of it is 'none of your money in the deal' deals. We will go on to look at the techniques of these strategies in the following chapters. I am not going to explain NMD in any more detail as it has been largely phased out. However, there are still a few dealers offering BMV deals.

Basically, if you are offered a property investment deal where you only have to pay £3,000–£5,000 plus or minus fees, consider the contract in detail. How is the deposit that the lender wants to be paid being paid? What level of gearing (loan to value in real terms) are you committed to and what is your cashflow?

Remember that one thing is guaranteed – interest rates will go up... Property prices are unlikely to move significantly, except possibly in London. How are you going to sustain this portfolio until you achieve capital growth or want to sell? How are you going to pay the mortgage when the rates go up or your tenant leaves?

Take advantage of your solicitor

Finding a good solicitor is an important part of any deal concerning the purchase of a property because you have to be confident that the solicitor is completely aware and totally competent in what they are doing and can overcome any obstacle. Your solicitor actual works for both you and the lender in the process of a property purchase.

So my advice would be to ask questions. Don't believe what people say just because they have been doing this longer than you. Ask as many questions as you need to. Ask your solicitor what they think. Be clear, honest and open with all of the information. Explain the deal to them and make sure they know all of the facts.

On a lighter note

Other options and strategies are available in the market to enable professional investors to keep buying property without using their own money. In other words, use other people's money to invest in property.

The following chapters in this book are filled with legal strategies that enable you to use other people's money. These include angel investors and family members, refurbishing and potentially even flipping.

My brush with fire

The following might explain why I am so against NMD deals. I blindly stumbled into a NMD deal after being recommended to a deal maker. I did not fully do my research on the deal and took the 'deal maker' at his word. He said that the lenders and solicitors were happy with the strategy. Note that I attempted this deal between June and August 2008 when lending was still at 85%, so it was theoretically a sweet deal that would actually give me cashback in my pocket after all costs. I definitely had greedy pound signs in my eyes and they blinded me, something which has driven a lot of investors towards this strategy.

It was my first solo purchase in Liverpool – a lovely three-bedroom mid-terrace with a slightly barmy vendor. I agreed a purchase price with 28% discount. That meant I agreed a sale price that was actually 72% of the original asking price.

This is not necessarily BMV. So, the first lesson for me was to understand what figure I was meant to be getting a discount on. Was it the market value and in whose opinion, mine or the surveyors? Or was the discount on the asking price?

The plan was that the deal maker would act as the purchaser (stay with me here), then I would buy the property from the deal maker-cum-new-vendor at the full original asking price. This was a higher figure than the actual agreed sale price. By doing this, I would effectively gain a mortgage on the full valuation rather than the discounted sale price.

OK, so that's the theory. Now I don't know how the deal maker was planning to fund his end of the purchase or what he was planning to do about the capital gains liability (that may have been covered in the £5,000 fees).

I had to apply for a £100,000 mortgage, using specified solicitors. There was some chaos here as I told my broker what was happening and he asked me to stop explaining because if he knew the full details he would have to inform the lender.

I got my mortgage offer and, as it was a relatively new experience for me, I read the terms and conditions of the offer. Mortgage Express clearly stated that the property had to be owned for a minimum of six months by the vendor. So, one week before exchange and after 20 stressful calls to the broker, deal maker, solicitors, estate agent, etc. the mortgage offer was withdrawn and a new mortgage had to be found at short notice – costing a second survey and associated fees.

The deal was no longer NMD as the technique had failed. I ended up leaving £20,000 in the deal and being tied into a mortgage for three years at 6.99%. Need I explain more? The vendor, the estate agent and me, of course, were stressed. Fees were wasted, over 10 weeks lost and a rubbish mortgage product grabbed at short notice. Never again...

Be safe – your future investing business and credit rating are at risk if you don't know what you are getting into and ignorance is no excuse.

Let's move on to some more chapters where you can use other people's money legally. Let's start close to home...

Chapter 6

Staying close to home – borrowing money from family and friends

Borrowing money from family and friends seems a great way to get started. Working with family and friends can also become the perfect practice for when you want to start working with angel investors later on in your career. Alternatively, working with angel investors can give you the discipline to work professionally with your family.

There are definitely pros and cons associated with borrowing money from family and friends. Some people are reluctant to do so as they feel awkward asking for money, but it is an easy way of getting into the property market. It also provides a great opportunity for the family member or friend to make a better rate of return on the money than they would if it was in the bank. It is really about sharing wealth and opportunities.

Start with an agreement

It is a good idea to draw up a formal agreement right from the start so that everyone involved in the investment deal knows what to expect, when to expect it and it simply makes things less complicated. The level of formality of the agreement is often dictated by the closeness of the family member and not necessarily the amount of money being borrowed. I would at the very least recommend that you just write down what you have agreed.

What should be in the agreement?

Don't make the conditions of borrowing the money over complicated. Start by understanding your deal. Are you planning to buy, refurbish and hold the property as a long-term buy-to-let, with the potential to remortgage and release funds in the next 6–12 months? Or are you planning to buy a property that needs a lot more work, significantly increase its value and then sell (flip) on?

Why does this matter? Well, think about how and when you are going to pay back the money you have borrowed and how much interest, if any, will be paid and when. The strategy you are planning to use will dictate the terms of your offer to any potential investor.

If you are planning to buy, do up and sell, for example, you could reach an agreement where you repay the money on the sale of the property. We would suggest that you also put a fixed and final date at some point in the future for the security of the investor.

In many cases where close family members are lending smaller amounts of money there is no conversation about interest payments. Especially if borrowing from parents who will often be more than willing to lend the money – unless of course you've not been a good son or daughter!

Where family or friends have a larger amount of money to lend, maybe taking the money from a savings account or releasing it as equity (see Chapter 7, page 47), then there needs to be a discussion about how working with you will generate more interest for them than a bank or building society. And, of course, you must cover the cost of any borrowing (in the example of equity release).

Again, at this point a simple document stating your names, the amount of the loan, the purpose of the loan, end/repayment date and any interest due is such an easy thing to do.

What if your best-laid plans go wrong?

If you are borrowing from one family member or friend, then this should be a relatively easy list of tasks to complete – make note of and keep a copy each. Think about having something in place in case of a falling out between partners (disagreement). Could the family member demand the money back? Make it clear in writing what the terms and conditions are for every eventuality.

A get-out clause will hopefully never be necessary because part of the process and discussion to create the terms of the agreement will show up any potential areas of disagreement. It is vital to your business' success that those people you do business with add to your success and do not detract from your profit.

I worked with a client recently who was an experienced investor with a medium-sized portfolio. He had bought property with family money and the help of a family member. After changes in the family, including divorce and death, the nature of the relationship changed and the family partner wanted their money back.

The investor came to me for ideas on how to raise the money needed to buy out the family member and get rid of all the stress. The detail of what I suggested is not important – the fact that I helped the investor see that they could increase the cashflow and pay off the family member was a great outcome. The lesson? Even family can fall out!

Now I am going to get morbid

As this money is being borrowed from family and/or friends, in my opinion, you should consider a life insurance policy and maybe even changes to your will. The principle here is not to leave your family in a mess should something unfortunate happen to you. If your daughter had taken out a loan on your behalf or your sister had lent you her savings, would you want them to be out of pocket, even if it was just for a matter of months while the probate was sorted out? It doesn't have to be expensive. Get a simple fixed term life insurance policy quote on the web.

Understanding the deal is the key

Really this is the easiest way to borrow money – you just need to understand your deal, what (how much) you need to get in and how you are planning to get out, your exit strategy. Then present your proposal to people.

A privately written finance document, or investor pack, can be used to write down and present, professionally, the details of the deal and why the deal would work. Most family members won't even read the document, but it will give you the confidence that you have thought through the deal and that their money is safe.

If you look at the maths, you will see just how easy borrowing money from friends and family can be. Imagine that you need £50,000 to pay for the deposit and all the purchasing costs of a property. To ask one person to lend you £50,000 might be a challenge, not only for you, but also for your family member or friend. There are definitely fewer people around with a full £50,000 lying around unused.

Now imagine that a combination of family members (say five to make my maths easy) all lend you £10,000 each. You still have the sum required. Each lender has either spread their risk or lent a smaller amount. Also, if at any point one investor needs their funds back, you only have to replace £10,000 and not a much larger amount. Do you know five people who might be interested in lending you money and earning a higher rate of interest than they would get in a bank?

Our agreement

In my case, I thought through as many variations and eventualities as possible. My family and I created a partnership agreement that clearly laid out how much money each family member put into the 'pot', what the money could be spent on, how profit would be shared. We discussed what would happen to the investments if one partner died. We made wills and put them into trust, then agreed that the wills would pay the beneficiaries. Then we agreed what would happen if one partner or investor wanted to leave the agreement before the time agreed. OK, it did take us more than a couple of hours, but that was because there was a lot we all had to consider, contribute and agree. In the end, we not only had a strong partnership but also a reasonable pot of money with which to start investing.

Case study 1

Mother and son – teamwork

This is a classic example where Mum started with a lump sum that was just sitting waiting in a bank for the right investment opportunity.

If you think of the primary strategy as using other people's money to invest in property to gain a much better rate of return than if the money simply sat in the bank, then investing in property exploits this strategy perfectly.

The 'secondary investment strategy' was to buy two to three three-bedroom properties and increase the number of bedrooms through redevelopment – creating an extra bedroom and the perfect multi-let (HMO) property. They quickly identified, bought and renovated two properties giving them a great cashflow. The HMOs give on average of £400 profit a month, this is seriously in excess of any bank returns! The properties are also worth more now than when they bought them; partly because of general renovation, but specifically because they have added an additional bedroom to each house.

They have cashflow, equity, future capital growth and of course a better ROI. They then went on to use the original cash lump sum to fund the redevelopment of a property bought specifically to 'flip' or sell on.

This new strategy means that they are in effect their own angel investors. They are using a combination of bank lending (mortgage), private finance (themselves) and credit cards to redevelop properties that should yield a profit of £30,000 plus within a three to six-month project window. Once the original investment is returned plus their profit, they can source and develop a new opportunity.

Case study 2

Stealth millionaires in the making

Borrowing from friends and family is often termed as a soft loan because the family member may not apply the same business head as a professional lender. They are also less likely to take enforcement action for repayment.

In 2010, one couple's sister and her husband were dependent on their savings, which were producing measly returns in the building society. They were going to be dependent on this money (return) for another five years until the husband could draw his pension.

The sister was not interested in investing in property, but was prepared to lend the investing couple £14,000 to fund their buy-to-let investment purchase and then lent a further £20,000 for the next. This was done without any security being offered, with the agreement done via email and purely on the strength of family trust. It is a big responsibility and 8% interest makes this cheap money.

The investors soon realised that they could easily raise some serious money within the family, as both sides of the family are savers and savers aren't exactly being well compensated at the moment. It hasn't gone unnoticed that they are getting better with every deal they do. Who saves in your family?

Chapter 7

Release money from your house (equity release)

'Equity release' is a term that means to release (through mortgage or remortgage) money (equity) from your own home, or another family member's home. This is possible where the current value of your mortgage is considerably less than the current value of your home. So, for example, if you bought your house a few years ago and have an outstanding £50,000 mortgage and the house is now worth £250,000, then there is up to £200,000 equity in the home that could be released.

Now, think back to Chapter 2 and the philosophy of Kiyosaki who believes in utilising your assets. Exploiting the leverage this strategy offers and using it to purchase other properties is exactly what he is talking about. This, like all of the other strategies, can be combined to make ever more creative deals, but let's keep it simple for now. It does take some thought and some planning, but is by far the easiest way to use other people's money to invest in property.

It pays for itself

In the ultimate of all 'none of your own money in the deal' deals – using other people's money – this strategy actually enables you to borrow the funds against your home or family member's home. You will know the effective cost of borrowing or using that money in advance, because it will have been released through a mortgage or further advance.

You can also calculate the cashflow from the proposed investment deal and make sure that it can cover that cost of borrowing. This should leave a surplus or profit. In effect, this strategy enables you to fund deposits on great cashflowing deals.

By using other people's money or releasing equity from your own house, you can increase the size of your property portfolio. By gaining control of another asset and collecting the additional cashflow, you leverage money from the bank to put additional funds into your pocket. Eventually, you repay the original loan using the capital gain as property prices inevitably increase in value.

The other 'selling' point for equity release is the leverage of your own home. How does this work? Your house will continue to slowly and gradually increase in value. That money or value is meaningless unless you release it through a sale or an equity release.

This, again, is where understanding good and bad debt is essential. I know I have visited hundreds of houses that were bought for £30,000 three or five years ago. I can see, using Hometrack[5], that they have been revalued and remortgaged. I can also see when I go in the house that they have had a new kitchen fitted and bought a flat screen TV. I also know that within 12–18 months of the remortgage they have been repossessed!

Why? Because that remortgage or equity release was bad debt; the money was spent on items that did not generate income to contribute towards paying off the interest due. I know what you are shouting… 'The kitchen added value to the house!' Well, maybe, but if they did not release the additional value and pay back the debt, as a professional investor would have done, then all they have done is treated themselves to a new luxury kitchen. Good debt is where the money borrowed is used to leverage more income over and above the cost of borrowing.

Good debt

The money you release must be and will be good debt. Surely you would only commit your own home or that of your parents when you knew for certain that the rental income would pay the interest and leave you with a surplus. You also need to know that you can remortgage the new investment properties in 6–12 months and pay back or recycle the funds into more cashflowing deals.

Remember that this cash from the equity release is being used to fund the purchase of undervalued properties. Depending on the level of access that you have to cash, you may be using the money as a deposit and then waiting 12 months (or six if you have commercial lending in place).

---

5   Hometrack is an online tool that enables you to search valuation and sale prices for a specific property or postcode.

Alternatively, if you have a sufficient equity pot, you may be buying outright and either flipping or remortgaging in six months on to the open buy-to-let mortgage market.

Remember that assets are things that give you a regular cashflow; when looking at a deal you should look for the cashflow and not just for the potential capital gain.

Interest rates, cashflow and release – they are the rules

Always do your research on the interest rates thoroughly for any money you plan to borrow through equity release. The property that you are considering releasing equity from will mostly likely already have a mortgage. If not, then just get the best rate possible. However, if it is mortgaged, then you need to understand the product you are on; your broker can help with this.

Don't be too quick to remortgage as you may lose a very preferential rate and end up costing yourself a lot of money over time. Working with your parents or older family members will be easier, as they will most likely be mortgage free.

Now invest wisely and always look for the cashflow. This is obvious but all the more important when you must use the surplus cashflow to cover the cost of the equity release as well as provide you with a profit. And always make sure you have a plan of when and how you will get the money back. If you are involving other family members, make sure they know you are doing it as a professional. Ensure that you have taken out suitable life insurance and put it in trust to protect the people you have borrowed money from.

It is important to understand where you want to be in five years' time. A good business strategy and a good exit strategy are crucial.

Creating money out of nothing

Just to drive the point home, in my case, I released just under £200,000 and used the money to fund seven purchases. Each property gives a minimum of £250 positive cashflow per month – that's a total cashflow of £1,750 per month. The cost of releasing the equity, i.e. the mortgage payment, is just under £500 per month, which means I have a net profit of £1,250 per month.

Let me explain our strategy for using other people's money in this way. We released £200,000 from my parents' unencumbered house. The cost of the mortgage was approximately £500 per month. I then used the £200,000 to fund the deposit and purchase costs of seven investment properties. The deposit and total purchase costs including broker, through solicitor, various fees and the refurbishment budget came to just under £30,000 per property. This also covered the cost of letting the property – all the certificates, letting agent fees and two months of mortgage costs, which is the maximum time I allow to refurbish and fill a property (although sometimes this can occur within a week).

Each of these properties is let, netting a profit of £250–£300 per month after the cost of the main mortgage, the letting agent fee and insurance. (In total, this is the mortgage plus about a 15% budget.) This surplus, on average £250, then contributes towards the initial cost of borrowing the £200,000 investment pot. The total overall profit across all seven properties is £1,250 per month. Let me just say that one more time – I make £1,250 profit from mortgaging my parents' house. And this is only one example.

I am just in the process of talking to two clients who are thinking about and planning for retirement.

Case study 1

Funding a peaceful retirement

A single lady with grown-up children and a current unencumbered house wants to move to her dream house in the next year. So, rather than sell her current home at a low point in the market, I have costed out that she can release £150,000 that would be covered by rental income. With the £100,000 she can invest in a property that will generate £1,000–£1,500 of rental profit and will pay the mortgage on the new home (using the £50,000 as a deposit). The challenge and solution is both her age and her children.

She is just about to create a property portfolio for herself (rental income) and her children and grandchildren (through the assets) of two main residential properties and two to four buy-to-let investment properties. In the long term, they can be moved into a family trust for the grandchildren. Best of all she lives rent free – forever!

Case study 2

Taking care of family

In the second example my client needs to care for elderly relatives. By investing the equity released from the family home, they can pay for the care needed and still retain assets and options. So the money released from the family home will be invested in buy-to-let property. The income (profit) generated will cover the cost of the care home fees. The younger members of the family can become involved with the property as co-mortgagees to give the bank security. The older members of the family can relax.

In addition, the home is still retained so should circumstances change they have the flexibility to move back in or sell in years to come.

Paying it back

Staying with the example of my parents' house for a moment, each property is on a one or two-year mortgage product. As each property becomes eligible for remortgage, I will check the valuations and, if sensible (because property values have increased), I will remortgage and then either repay the mortgage on my parents' house or more likely reinvest the money into yet more properties.

Given the property market, house prices (which fell slightly in 2010 and early 2011) and general unpredictability of anything, I am only budgeting to get back part of the funds invested. I have calculated that if prices don't rise, but 75% loan to value (LTV) is still available, then any property bought 20% under value will mean that the cost of the mortgage can mostly be recouped. The cost of purchase, refurbishing and letting (approximately £5,000–£10,000) will still be in the deal. Even with £10,000 in the deal that would still mean over 20% ROI (see Chapter 17).

How does the equity release owner benefit?

Now if you consider my strategy described above, you could offer your family member a share of that profit. If you share, for example a 70/30 split, you personally could still net £875 a month and your family or friend take £375 a month.

In my case, I pay a 'fee' each time I use the money, as splitting the profit, which was small in the first instance, didn't seem such a great offer. The 'lending fee' is a tax-deductible expense to the business. As long as I keep the annual total paid to my parents under their tax-free allowance, then they don't pay tax either – a win-win situation for all involved.

OK, so what's the risk?

We have been taught by parents and peers to pay our mortgages off and that debt is bad, but, as you know, it is important to make the distinction. Some people, quite rightly, have concerns about releasing equity from a property, especially if it is your own home or your parents' home.

It can also involve some legal paperwork to sign deeds over from one person to another, so that there is an income-earning person on the mortgage. It can make partners who are not educated in the ways of professional property investing feel really uncomfortable and afraid about the future security of their home.

This can all be easily resolved by seeing a financial advisor or a solicitor who will be able to explain that the release is to invest in assets that are income generating. Also, the use of the private finance document can help you to clarify and explain the property proposal and demonstrate past experience or show examples.

Now a word of caution

You are actually putting yourself in a position where your deal is 100% funded. This means you really must ensure that you have excellent cashflow to cover the cost of the two loans.

Personally, I would still want to be receiving at least £200 per month per property after the main (buy-to-let) mortgage, the equity release mortgage and insurance, etc. have all been paid. Remember, my properties only attract £500 per month rent – so work this up for your strategy. Use ROI as a measure and get 10–14% coverage.

You may be wondering why am I setting the figure so high. This is because interest rates have never been better; the Bank of England is at 0.5% and can only go up. So if you can't get good cashflow now, then maybe the deal isn't good enough. After all, the whole point of this is to get cash flowing into your pocket!

The other concern is that in the early part of 2012, LIBOR started to rise. Some lenders were offering products linked to LIBOR. When banks lend you money they have had to borrow it from somewhere first. They borrow money based on LIBOR, so they need to make a profit on the money they borrow and hence the cost of lending becomes linked explicitly or implicitly to LIBOR. As it rises, so too will the true cost of our borrowings – beware!

Chapter 8

Turning Cinders into Cinderella – refurbishing and releasing equity

Building on the last model of releasing equity, this strategy revolves around the equity release from the investment property itself. This strategy is both similar and different to that in Chapter 7. The biggest difference is that you need to remortgage and this may be possible in six months or may not be possible for a year. This exit plan will need funding through either credit cards or a family or friend loan.

Critical success factors

Making this work depends on four factors. I will outline these in brief and then explain in more detail:

1. **Picking the right area** – if you are planning to sell or remortgage, you need to be in an area where the 'ceiling' price of the road does not limit your potential profit.

2. **Having the right team**, from estate agent contacts to builders who can work to the right level of specification (spec).

3. **Knowing the numbers**. Like in the previous chapters, understanding the numbers of this deal are crucial. This strategy involves not only the purchase price, but also the cost of the refurbishment and a small error in judgement here can be very costly.

4. **Getting the money back out** – what are your two exit strategies?

Picking the right area

This strategy, along with the buy, refurbish and sell (flip) strategy, needs the property to be in a desirable area with potential market growth. There are hundreds, if not thousands, of derelict and boarded properties in the north of England and, yes, they will be cheap. Unfortunately, no amount of money spent on them will enable you to get your investment back because the area, and the market in that area, will not enable you to raise the value sufficiently that you will get your money back out or be able to sell quickly for a good price.

You will find areas where this works, but you need to do your research and know the market. You will need to buy at a significantly low price in order to meet this equation.

Final valuation x 75% = loan. The loan – cost of refurbishment and purchase costs – must equal or be more than the price you pay for the property.

If you speak to estate agents about a property before you buy it, you can pretend that you are thinking of selling. (Obviously you need to speak to a different agent to the one who is selling to you!) Ask them what the 'ceiling price' for the street is. What is the highest sale price currently being achieved and what has it reached in the past (before the crash)? This should help you to recognise the maximum price that you will achieve on sale or remortgage. It is tough to achieve ceiling price and even harder to break though. Go for the easily achievable prices, even slightly under market value.

Having the right team

A good way to find properties that are for sale, at less than market value, is to develop a relationship with estate agents. Some property trainers give the impression that you can just go to an estate agency, walk in the door, offer 30% below market value or asking price and walk out with the deal.

In my experience, and talking to other professional investors, this is far from the truth. Estate agents get loads of people walking in saying 'I am a professional investor. Can I have a good deal?' The reality is that if the agent is any good, they will already have a discrete client list of people who they have built relationships with over time.

In order to get estate agents' attention you will need to be professional, consistent and trustworthy. Never make an offer on a property if you do not intend to follow through. Stay in regular contact, go to viewings and talk to them about your strategies. Along with estate agents, RightMove and local papers are great places to find potential properties. If you are looking near your own home, get to know your local properties, watch for houses that have been on the market a long while and look for run down and empty properties.

This also applies to working with builders – a good relationship is crucial. However, don't get complacent as you still need to check quotes. In an ideal situation, you would develop a niche and a model that you keep repeating. Once you achieve this, you can effectively keep a build team permanently busy. This ensures their success and loyalty and guarantees the quality of your product.

A little dramatic maybe, but whether you are planning to buy and renovate a property, to keep it or sell it, you will need the appropriate power team. The most important thing you need to know is what is the appropriate standard needed to rent a property quickly and what is the appropriate standard needed to sell a property quickly? These can be vastly different depending on the market you are targeting. Estate agents and letting agents are the best people to ask. Builders can also talk to you about refurbishment standards, but they may tell you what suits them in terms of how much they can charge you!

Even when you have an established relationship with your builders, kitchen companies and other trades people and suppliers, you should regularly check their prices are remaining competitive. Treat them well, pay them promptly and build a trusting relationship so you know you can rely on them. It is not always about going for the cheapest option, it is about achieving the best.

If you have found the right run-down house, the rough diamond in the area that with a bit of polish and tender loving care you can turn into a diamond, that is a great start. You have a tried and tested team or one recommended to you. Now you need to be clear about how you will fund and ultimately release those funds.

Rightmove is a well-known website that advertises property for sale or rent. It can be used to assess valuations and rentals. It is also possible to make assumptions about supply and demand in an area.

Knowing the numbers

When I buy a property I aim to get 50% or more of my cash back out, because I combine my investment strategy with my (using other people's money) finance strategy. This means that I am focused on cashflow, getting as much as possible as quickly as possible. I am a preferred landlord by tenants in my area (the bench mark is horrific, I have to say – most tenants living in cold, damp properties). I aim to provide a decent home, warm, dry, damp free. I do not routinely redecorate every room after every tenant leaves. I ask my tenants what they would like to do to the property and encourage them to make it their own.

So, I spend a small to medium budget on renovation. I have slightly higher ongoing maintenance costs, but the properties are rented quickly for a great return and then remortgaged to release 50% of cash invested after 12 months. In three to five years I will start a process of renovating the properties, subject to market conditions, to either increase the property through an extension or in order to sell a property a year for tax benefits.

Another approach is to fully renovate a property to a sale standard from day one. In my area this would incur £25,000–£30,000 upfront costs compared to £5,000 on average. And it also means that the property will not start generating rent until the work is completed – potentially three to four months down the line. Meanwhile, you will have to pay the mortgage. So I would want 100% of my funds returned.

A word of caution here: one person I spoke to invested in my area; bought in a postcode I would not touch and renovated over three months to a professional standard and created an HMO. HMOs in the north of England are frequently properties for single, unemployed men with multiple issues such as alcohol, drugs or mental health issues. Professionals want access to work and transport. So, wrong property strategy, wrong location and wrong refurbishment strategy.

Another example is that developing a property to sale standard means you must be aware of the wider area plans. What does the council have in store for an area? Will this help or hinder your sale?

What will other buyers find when they do the search? I was speaking with one lady who found a deal with a single-storey extension. There are all sorts of pitfalls here, not least changes in the energy performance standards, which will come into effect and become law over the coming years. Think carefully.

Getting the money back out

At present, the lenders are taking the view that a property bought and sold in under six months is obviously suspicious and many will not lend to the buyer (or remortgagor). There is no point in listing which companies will or will not currently lend to you in under that time and what their conditions are, because it changes so frequently.

The general principle is this – you will need two lenders; you will buy the house through one lender and then remortgage with a second lender. This is so that you can get a different surveyor to visit the property after you have renovated it and let them see it with new and clear eyes. Now, as the HBOS group seems to own most of the marketplace, you will need to plan this carefully. Know your lender and know their surveyors!

The other thing to consider is that each mortgage comes with conditions and often with 'tie-in' periods. You will need to get an initial mortgage with no 'early redemption penalties'. This first lender ideally needs to have a product with no or a very low tie-in period or fee. This is why a commercial loan is a perfect example. If you look hard and wide enough, you will find other building societies that also have no tie-ins. However, they may also only lend 60 or 65% of the purchase price. There is always a pay-off to be made.

You would then look for a second lender who is well placed in the market with a combination of high LTV and lower interest rates. Now the lender you choose to be your second and permanent lender may change their rates, their conditions and all sorts of other things before you get a chance to complete – so you will need to watch the market and be flexible.

For the last few years, one lender has been offering a 'light refurbishment product' so you will need a great mortgage broker. They can make or break your profit margin! Make sure you understand the numbers and the pros and cons of this product. The speed of equity release after the refurb is often off-set by the LTV. Certainly worth considering…

To get all your money back out with LTV at around 75%, you will need to be buying about 30% or more under market value. Obviously, you will need to speak to estate agents and letting agents in the area to find out rental costs and to surveyors about your end values. Have a look around the area where the property is, at both daytime and night time to get a feeling for the area. Speak to the neighbours to find out what the local area is really like. Do your research.

Case study

Cinders or Cinderella?

One really important thing to remember is that you are refurbishing your investment property for a purpose – for a specific tenant. Therefore, the work needs to result in a property that meets their tastes not yours. Valley was our first solo property within our joint venture partnership. Over the space of four days we managed to do more damage to the house and we delayed the rental of the property by a week, because we had to finish our unnecessary renovations.

What did we do? Well, the biggest and most costly mistake was to have not asked the letting agent what he thought we needed to do (as it was our first investment in a new area). Had we asked, he would have said, 'Add two cupboards in the kitchen and stop.'

What we did was take down the flowery border at the top of the walls in every room and, therefore, damaged the paintwork resulting in the redecoration of every room. We moved the sink in the bathroom from in front of the window to along the wall, which meant we also had to relocate the radiator, which in turn, meant lifting the carpet and floor boards!

This meant we had to buy fixtures and fittings, new bathroom flooring and, oh, we decided we didn't like the colour of the bathroom tiles – more expense!

You must know when you are working on a 'Cinders' that needs a full renovation and when you are buying a property that simply needs a partial refurbishment. Overall, remember that any money you invest must give you a return on that investment and that you are aiming to create a property that appeals to your prospective tenant or buyer, not yourself.

Now I have two builders; one I use if I am just letting the house because I know that I may have to repaint in a few months, but plan that my tenants like the property so much that they stay forever and paint the walls the colours they like. I use my second builder for properties in the more desirable areas of town and if I am planning to resell quickly.

When it comes to the point of sell or remortgage, I am building a cashflowing portfolio so I rarely sell a property other than for specific immediate cash gain or tax purposes. Personally, I have a number of properties that are due for remortgage and I have been waiting to see how the market performs before I commit too early. There has already been one increase in the LTV ratios and, therefore, it would be sensible to see what happens. I am negotiating with my bank and I am not currently at any disadvantage if I wait another month or two. Of course, this will depend on who lent you the initial deposit money and the terms of that agreement.

Chapter 9

Buy to sell – making every penny count

Know what you are planning to get into and get out of

Buying to sell is an attractive strategy to many people if your initial pot of investment funds is relatively small. You can use your pot of money strategically by selecting the refurbishment property that you are planning to work on with a laser-like focus on the end result. Put your money into the deal, pay for your refurbishment costs using an assortment of financial strategies, sell the completed project and then get your pot plus profit back out again.

However, buying to sell or 'buy, refurb and flip' is a very special game in today's challenging market. You will really need to understand your market, both as the buyer of a below market gem and as a vendor of a 'ready to move in' home. After all, you are selling to 'want-to-be' homeowners.

There are also more tax implications with this strategy as the sale produces a taxable profit – rather than cash released as debt through a remortgage which is tax free. While you can off-set this with your annual capital gains tax allowance, this is currently only £10,600 per person and once used is gone, it also can't be carried forward. This would work well if you have a large extended family who you trust. Otherwise, you will give up to 28% or more to the tax man. If you remortgage, the money released is tax free debt! I have attempted this strategy twice with a poor result (thank goodness for my second exit strategy!), so I personally feel the market is too volatile and that this is too high risk by my standards. Or maybe I mean the prices too static and the surveyors too volatile – you get my drift!

If you decide to pursue this strategy, there are lots of ways that you can finance a deal like this. For example, using bridging finance (from family and friends, a company or angel investor) to purchase the property, either outright or with a mortgage to cover 75%. Then use credit cards to do the refurbishment or maybe make an agreement with the builder to pay them at the sale of the property to cover the rest of the costs.

You can see already how this can be a more complex type of project using a blend of finance strategies. Of course, the investment strategy itself must be absolutely solid!

Making it work – worst house in the best street

The most crucial aspect of making this strategy work is:

- finding the right property
- getting your budget right
- managing your team
- perfecting your marketing.

Finding the right property is easy if you think of it this way: you want to find the worst house in the best street. This means that you can buy undervalue, add value (within a tightly controlled budget) and then sell at just under the ceiling price. Remember, every street will have a ceiling price and deciding to buck the trend may be more difficult (and costly) in a slower market.

If you are going to make this work, then you really need to make sure that you keep an eye on the timescales for your refurbishment so that your costs don't run too high. Budget properly for the tools and help needed for the refurbishment, as a mistake here will cost you your profit.

There is a risk that the refurbishment will take longer than you plan, especially with older properties. If your project overruns, it will eat into your profit. Most importantly, you will need to make sure that you can cover the cashflow required to cover the monthly costs whilst you are waiting for work to finish or the sale to go through. This is particularly important if you use bridging (see Chapter 10). A deal that slips into another month of bridging costs could cost you another £1,500 extra in bridging costs!

Making every penny count – manage your emotions, your team and your budget

The temptation with a property is to get emotionally involved in the deal – 'It's a lovely house'. No, it's not. It's a great business opportunity as long as you can stick to your plan. You will need to be sure that any refurbishment work or improvements that you carry out are actually going to add value to the house.

Don't go in and change things that don't necessarily need changing just because it is not to your taste (see Case study in Chapter 8, page 58). Kerb appeal is obviously something to think about, but once inside the house you need to know how much extra value adding another bedroom would bring.

The kitchen is always important – it needs to have enough room to move, enough cupboard space to store things, and be clean and tidy. The same considerations need to be applied to the bathroom. A neat trick for quick refurbishment is to re-mastic round the bath and the sink, replace the taps and then thoroughly clean. It is not always necessary to replace a bath suite – unless of course it is not white! Does it matter if the bathroom is downstairs or is that the norm for the area? Remember to tailor your product to your customer's taste, not yours!

Focus on the end result and market accordingly

The next thing to remember is: who is your client? A large three-bedroom house with only a shower not a bath could mean that families with young children will be put off. Is your potential buyer a first-time buyer or an investor? There is a difference between preparing a house for an investor to buy as a business and a member of the general public looking for a home.

Over cautious and pleasantly surprised

What do I mean by this? When undertaking a project like this, I carry out research to demonstrate the 'weakest' value of the property at purchase while also knowing the 'reasonable' potential sale price. By that I mean, never base your profit figures on the maximum sale prices in the area when calculating your figures.

You will also need to consider how much profit you want to make on a deal to make it worthwhile. Some people are happy to do deals for £10,000. Other investors would not look at a deal unless there was at least £40,000 profit in the project or a significant return (75-100%) on capital employed after all the costs.

So be overly cautious on your profit projections and then pleasantly surprised at an increased profit outcome, rather than horrified at a weak profit margin. Make allowances in terms of time (and cash) to cover the refurbishment and sale. For example, add a contingency budget of eight weeks – just in case. Also add between 10–20% contingency and overrun on the refurbishment costs (dependent on the size of the project). It is far better in my opinion to only expect £20,000 profit and then make £30,000, than to expect £30,000 but only make £20,000.

Marketing – what's the plan?

Think about how you are going to market the property. Will it be marketed with empty rooms or will it be marketed with furniture? How will the property be advertised? Will you be advertising it yourself, will you go through newspapers or websites or place it with an estate agent?

At what point in the refurbishment process can someone come and see the property? I bought a house where I saw it before the builder started work, and then saw it again while works were being carried out. Maybe you could enable the future homeowner to choose the colour scheme?

If you have bought the property through an estate agent, then why not stay in touch and offer them the new sale as part of your relationship-building strategy? You can then use the expertise of the local estate agent to guide and influence some of your refurbishment decisions.

On a new deal bought direct from the home owner, I asked my local estate agent to view the property and give me their opinion of essential works needed to ensure a quick sale. Then I invited the builder round to give me their opinion on the essential works needed to sell the house quickly to a specific target market. I made a judgement where the two lists differed – based on the cost of works and the potential return. Builders and estate agents will expect to get the business if the deal goes through. Think carefully about how you use their time and respect their businesses.

I would still advertise a property on websites and newspapers just to speed the selling process and maximise the rate of return of the initial money invested. Like any of the strategies I have talked about so far, you need to understand both the market you are operating in and the clients/tenants/ buyers or investors that will finally take possession of the property.

Case study

Redeveloping to order

I worked with a mentee to see how they could maximise the income from their portfolio. They were in a good position in terms of gearing – the overall portfolio was at 75%.

They wanted to see how they could raise more cash to continue investing.

My first questions were: how much cashflow did they have as a target; and where was the portfolio in terms of meeting that financially-free target figure?

As we examined strategies for each property and various combinations, it became clear they had one property that could be redeveloped. The challenge was they did not have the funds to pay for the work.

The property was in a highly desirable street. I set a list of research questions: was there a market (need) for the planned redevelopment? Would planning permission be granted? Once we knew there was a potential market and the project was feasible, we moved on to the costs involved: what would the potential resale value be (remember to under estimate)? What were the build costs? What were the solicitor and estate agent fees?

This project became a development deal where the vendor could influence the interior design of the finished project. How? They effectively bought the finished property through an exchange with delayed completion.

The buyer paid a deposit of 14% upfront (more than the usual 10%), which funded the cost of the redevelopment.

The final deal meant an uplift in value of £150,000 for a cost of £50,000 funded by the new owner. The profit is £100,000 plus the equity already in the property. The next phase of the plan is to invest in more cashflowing properties as that is the primary target. Expected cashflow increase to be over £1,000 pcm and counting.

Best time and lost time

Your budget and, therefore, profit will be based on a timescale (as mentioned previously). You must budget for overruns, as well as for extra interest costs and/or extra refurbishment costs. If the overall aim of this strategy is to buy at a discount and then make a profit, you need to know that every penny you spend will add value. I roughly calculate that the refurbishment work I am doing will mean each pound spent will generate at least £3 pounds of extra profit.

Finally, think about the economic environment. We all know that there are more popular times of the year to buy, everyone loves to buy when the sun is out. Look at your timescales and maybe rethink your plans if the timescale means that you will be going to market just after Christmas.

Speak to the estate agents about peak buying times in your area and work to that timescale. Above all, if you are planning to resell instead of remortgage, choose your property with your buyer in mind. See if you can find the potential buyer before you complete on your deal, therefore all refurbishment work would in effect be carried out to order, especially if they sign a contract stating that.

Chapter 10

Bridging loans – the last port in a storm

What is it and why do people use it?

Bridging finance or a bridging loan is basically short-term money borrowed for a specific business reason. A bridging loan is a formal agreement where either an individual or a company lends you money for a fee, for a period of time, which is secured against a property. This formal approach to borrowing other people's money is not a strategy I have personally used, though I have worked with mentees as they have progressed through deals.

So, in some ways, a 'bridge' or bridging loan is a mini mortgage used to bridge and span a short period of time before more permanent loans are put in place, such as a buy-to-let mortgage. Having used the words 'short period', I should explain this can be anywhere from one day to six to eight months (or longer – but then you really need to have a great reason to do this).

Bridging loan companies are not bound by the Council of Mortgage Lenders' rules and, therefore, do not lend according to purchase price. The bridging company is not always interested in lending just based on a percentage of the purchase price. They will consider lending based on a percentage of the value of the property.

A bridging company could be completely happy with lending 100% of the full purchase price. Though, typically, a bridging company would be prepared to lend 70% of the valuation or 100% of the purchase price whichever is lower. You may have agreed a purchase price of £65,000 on a property worth (according to valuation) £100,000, for example. Therefore, in this case, the bridging company would lend £65,000 as the purchase price is less than 70% of the valuation.

When bridging makes sense

Bridging finance is often used when a property is unmortgageable for some reason. Perhaps the property does not have a bathroom or a kitchen, so it is classed as uninhabitable. Another reason might be because the property transaction needs to complete quickly, such as when buying from an auction.

In the example of a property that is uninhabitable, the investor will have most likely proceeded to get a regular buy-to-let mortgage offer, but with a condition of a full retention until certain works are completed. They would then use bridging finance to buy the property, fit the kitchen or complete refurbishment works, and then ask the lender to reinspect and release funds to clear the bridge.

As with every method described in this book, the critical point is to know how you are going to repay the bridging loan. There are huge penalties for overrunning on the agreed timescales. Let's look at some of the costs involved.

So what is it going to cost – one arm or two legs?

Bridging loans are notoriously expensive. Interest is calculated on a daily or monthly interest rate. So, for example, you may be offered 1.5–2%, but this is actually approaching 18–24% per annum. Quite a shock when a buy-to-let mortgage would cost approximately 5% per annum.

How do the numbers actually work?

Most bridging companies will charge for the following:

- Arrangement fee – this is typically 2% of the loan, a one-off upfront payment.
- Legal and admin costs – usually £500–£1,000, which covers the bridging company's legal fees – you will still need to budget for your own costs.
- Ongoing interest – this can range from 1.25–2% a month. Of course, how you pay the interest is entirely down to the company and negotiation. It can be paid monthly, but most experienced investors will look to get an agreement to have the 'interest rolled up'. This means the interest will accrue and you will settle the loan and the charges at the end of the period.
- Exit costs – there is typically an exit fee that is one month's interest of the loan. However, there are some bridging companies that do not charge this fee – it is worth checking.

How interest is charged

Most bridging companies charge interest on a monthly basis, which means if you use your bridge for two months and one day, you will be charged three months' interest. However, there are some flexible bridging companies that charge interest on a daily basis. It's worth looking out for these firms, as they tend to work out cheaper in the long term, especially if you are renovating and you are ahead of schedule.

So do the figures work for you?

As you can see, bridging loans can work out very expensive. Sometimes it's worth it and sometimes it's not. As an investor, you need to know that you can afford the monthly fees associated with having a bridging loan, which could quite easily be around £2,000 a month on a typical £100,000 loan.

You will also need to be very aware that any overrun in the project refurbishment or delay in a sale will impact significantly on your profit, and may even wipe it out completely!

If you exceed the term of your bridging loan, the interest can double.

What is the catch? (Apart from the cost)

- How are you getting the money back to the bridging company? The first question any bridging company will always ask is: 'What is your exit strategy?' This means they want to know how you are going to pay them their money back. Why do they ask this – because they only want you to have their money for a short amount of time, which enables them to lend the money back out to someone else and make more money.
- Nine times out of 10, if you can convince a bridging company that they can get their money back in a reasonable amount of time, typically six to eight months, they will lend you the money.
- So what exit strategy do they want to see? Principally, that you have been pre-approved for a buy-to-let mortgage, which will in effect buy out their debt.

- Experience. In many cases, the company will want to see that you have a track record as an experienced investor and so this particular strategy is not always available as your first approach to using other people's money to invest in property. Some bridging companies will want you, as an individual wanting to borrow money, to have experience in investing with three to five investment properties already in your portfolio as reassurance, but not always.

- Timescale. As an investor, you would need to show what you want to use the money for and how long you need it. It usually takes 5–10 days to receive the funds once your request for a bridging loan has been approved. This will include a survey on the property.

- Use a financial advisor. The bridging company is there primarily to lend money and make a profit. They are not financial advisors, although some financial advisors also lend money through a bridging company. You should speak to your financial advisor to check that you are making a sound financial decision to go ahead and invest using bridging finance.

- Your advisors and the bridging company will then carry out the normal due diligence on you, your strategy and the property. Ultimately, the bridging company needs to be sure that you are able to keep up and manage the loan repayments before they lend you the money (if you are paying the interest on a regular monthly basis).

- Security. As mentioned already, the bridging company will require adequate security; this may take the form of a charge on your home, a charge on the property you wish to buy or a number of properties in your investment portfolio.

- This provides a level of 'comfort' to the lender. Make no mistake, if you do not pay on time, they will move to repossess the security they hold a legal charge on. So be very careful about the terms of the deal you agree.

Where do they get the money to lend?

It really depends on the bridging company. Some use their funds from a pot of money they hold, and some have funding lines with major financial institutions like high street banks. There are other companies that use money lent to them.

Bridging companies may use money lent to them by savvy members of the general public. For example, someone could have come into some capital and identified that they have a lump sum of money that they are not going to use for six or seven months or even two to three years. They would talk with the finance company and discuss what opportunities are available to invest in at the moment.

The savvy investor would receive half of the upfront fee, 10% per month and half of the exit fee, which is a significant proportion of fees and a great return on their investment. This is considerably more than they would get from a bank or building society. Of course, there is the risk that there could be an overrun and they may not receive the payment when it is due, but the bridging company's role is to mitigate against this happening.

Specific and specialist

This strategy is used to support a specific investment approach. For example, I have a contact who buys property at auction, uses his build team to renovate the property and then resells the property to other investors or to the general public.

By using bridging finance and selling deals in this way you could still be a property trader, where the size of your portfolio, or lack of equity in your portfolio, limits your ability to access additional mortgage lending. Bridging does not hinder the sale of the property because you are not tied into fixed-term mortgage products. There are definite advantages.

Disadvantages come in the form of huge financial penalties for overstepping an agreed time frame – so do your calculations precisely and then factor in some extra time because these things always take longer than they are meant to. Good luck!

Chapter 11

Freehold-leasehold: the parts are greater than the sum

What makes this strategy so clever?

By buying a property that is actually just a 'lump' of flats you can generate a lot of cash-generating exit strategies. First, for example, you could keep all four flats and make four times the cashflow. Or you could sell one or two flats and have both the benefit of cashflow and future capital appreciation from those you keep while generating some immediate cash lump sums from those you sell. Or you could sell three flats and essentially get one flat for yourself for free.

This is only made possible if you get your power team and your numbers right. The variations and opportunities are endless and highly profitable if you:

- find the right deal
- have an expert solicitor and experienced broker
- get the vendor on side
- build up a rapport with a local letting agent with experience
- have a great deal of nerve.

Above all, it is about understanding the strategy, working out the combination of funding structures and knowing where and how the money will be made in the deal.

Freehold-leasehold?

'Freehold-leasehold' is a common commercial strategy often seen when there are flats above a shop. Let's start with the term 'freehold' – this is the term for the title of a property. In other words, the Queen who owns England gives you permission to build on her land without additional charges. So you own the free holding of the land and the properties on it.

'Leasehold' means that you own only the bricks and mortar and you effectively are renting or leasing the land from the freeholder. In return, they charge you rent (usually something small like £100 per annum; in the old days a peppercorn was used, hence the term 'peppercorn rent').

Houses can be leasehold properties and the freeholder in the case of a single dwelling will simply charge the ground rent and that is all. In the case of a multiple dwelling, like flats, the freeholder will have responsibilities to maintain the exterior of the building and all the common areas. They will pass this cost on to you.

What does a freehold-leasehold look like?

A typical property would be a Victorian townhouse that had been converted into flats many years ago. It could also look like an ordinary house. It is very unlikely to be new build or a bungalow.

It must have an 'established use' meaning that the flats have been in existence long enough that the utility companies and post office recognise them as separate entities. Of course, the whole building must be for sale; otherwise you are just buying a few flats. So there is this contradiction of the building being considered as one entity, just one property as far as land registry is concerned, while the component flats have been in practical use for so long that the utility companies see the building as separate flats.

Listings for this type of building can be found at auctions, with estate agents or on RightMove. It is a more complex purchase, often involving the purchase of three or more component flats at the same time. Ordinary investors will neither have the skills nor understanding to complete on these purchases.

You will need to prepare, and a good idea may be to have a checklist of what to look out for. These include things like planning permission, which can be checked out with the local council in the early stages of your research. You will need to know whether planning permission to change the 'house' into flats was obtained and, if so, how long ago.

Next, you will need to know if each unit or flat has its own front door, gas and electricity supply, kitchen, bathroom/toilet and bedroom. The property must be a recognisable flat in itself – a separate dwelling in its own right. If not, you will have to install this and that will mean a full renovation budget.

Getting the power team

Unlike previous chapters where it was the builder who was so important, in this strategy you need to have an experienced solicitor who understands and has dealt with this type of purchase before. The solicitor will need to be experienced in splitting the freehold into leases. You will also need an accountant or go online and set up a Limited Company, and at some point you will be trading these properties, which means you'll need an experienced broker or commercial mortgage arrangement.

Your broker will need to know which lenders are happy to lend on this type of deal. In this model you will be creating new leases and essentially buying newly leased properties and some lenders don't like that at the moment. It falls into the six-month trap as the new lease and the purchase from the Limited Company essentially mean that the property will not have been owned by the immediate vendor for six months.

You will also need to have a number of different lenders involved because no one lender will want to feel overexposed by lending on the whole property. So, for example, in a property consisting of four established flats you will need to find four lenders who are prepared to lend on newly created leases!

You may also need to ask family or friends to hold the mortgages for you if your credit availability is low. If you have 10 or more buy-to-let properties, this may add an additional challenge for your broker.

Getting the vendor and occupiers on side

Then, of course, you really need to consider the vendor as part of your power team because they have the power to enable the deal or not. Each component part or flat will need to be visited at least three times; first by you, then by a mortgage surveyor and then by an architect who will draw the plans needed to create the leases. As you can imagine, this might inconvenience any tenants in the property, as they will need to either provide keys and give access permission or be present at every viewing. All the component parts will need to be viewed.

You will also need to make sure that the mortgage surveyors do not meet or hear about the architect and, therefore, preferably not meet the tenants either. The mortgage surveyor just needs to value the flats and not worry about the future creation of leases. This whole process can cause major time delays and your vendor will need to understand this is not going to be the world's quickest purchasing system.

Making the numbers work – part 1

As with all investment deals, it is important to do your research on your target property and make sure the numbers work out in your favour (i.e. profitably) before viewing at all. When we talk about the figures involved in these deals, it is slightly different from a regular buy-to-let investment.

You are looking for a property where 75% of the final value of the component flats (because you will get a 75% LTV mortgage for example) equals or exceeds the cost of the original freehold property purchase price, the buying costs (solicitors, surveys, etc.) and the cost of any building or refurbishment works needed. If this works, then you will have found yourself one of the ultimate NMD deals.

Let me go over these numbers again and why it is the ultimate NMD deal. Let's pick an easy example. The freehold property is worth £300,000 (and you pay the asking price just to make it easy). The house was split into four self-contained one-bedroom flats about 15 years ago. A separate one-bedroom flat is easily worth £100,000.

See how easy I am making the maths? It really does not work out quite so simply in real life, but hopefully you will get the point of the strategy and then explore for yourself.

So when you split the title into four separate one-bedroom flats and get four separate mortgages at 75% LTV – you will have a mortgage 'cash pot' of 4 x £75,000 which equals £300,000, the cost of the purchase price.

Now, if you get a better purchase price or better valuations on the final flats, then you will also get enough money through on the mortgages to cover the purchase costs and maybe any renovations required

Let me do another example with slightly different figures to help you understand further.

Making the numbers work – part 2

In the example in the diagram on page 77 you will see that the freehold property is being sold for £300,000. Once you have built up a rapport with

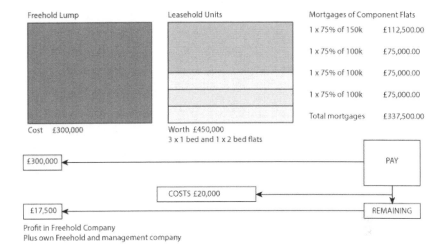

Freehold Lump

Cost £300,000

Leasehold Units

Worth £450,000
3 x 1 bed and 1 x 2 bed flats

Mortgages of Component Flats

1 x 75% of 150k	£112,500.00
1 x 75% of 100k	£75,000.00
1 x 75% of 100k	£75,000.00
1 x 75% of 100k	£75,000.00
Total mortgages	£337,500.00

£300,000 ← PAY

COSTS £20,000 ←

£17,500 ← REMAINING

Profit in Freehold Company
Plus own Freehold and management company

the estate agent, you will be able to negotiate confidently in the knowledge that there will be plenty of viewings but not many offers, as few investors know how to make this type of deal work.

You will be able to calculate the value of the leasehold units through plenty of research. Always assume the lowest component values to be extra cautious. Again, speak to your broker and know what loans and LTVs you can get on all four flats (in this example).

On the bright side, if you buy the place for £275,000 and get valuations on the three one-bedroom flats at £120,000 each, then your profit would soar to £87,500 instead of just £17,500.

On the gloomy side, if the mortgage on the two-bedroom flat comes in at 70% LTV (giving a mortgage of £105,000) and your cost calculations were wrong meaning you need to spend £40,000 instead of £20,000, then you would have to put £10,000 in the deal or sell one or more of the flats. Knowing the numbers inside and out is critical to the success of this strategy and that is why cautious valuations on your part are an absolute must.

However, if the deal did cost you £10,000 (providing you could access the funds), that would work out as £2,500 per flat which is still a bargain. Some investors will use this strategy even if they do have to put money in the deal because it can be a very cheap way of acquiring flats and, therefore, cashflow.

Chapter 12

Lease options – pros and cons

The problem with lease options

First, I will briefly explain what a lease option is… with a lease option you are not taking on a debt, you are effectively asking a person to lease you their house. You then 'ask' for permission from the homeowner and their lender to rent out the property. The new tenant pays rent and effectively pays for the existing mortgage cost on the property; just the same as in a traditional purchase – except you do not have a debt – the homeowner still has the mortgage debt in their name. You are a letting agent!

The 'option' part is where you also get the owner of the property to agree to sell you the property at a point in the future for a price agreed today. This is where most people see the cash is to be made in the deal.

The fact is that they are gambling on property prices. If the deal works in their favour, then they have control of a property with no mortgage, potential cashflow (we'll come to that) and then the chance to make a 'fortune' when the property prices increase and they enact their option at a much lower price, as agreed.

The issues for me are:

1. Who is likely to agree to this sort of deal?

2. What are your rules for what makes a good deal?

3. What if property prices do not go up or don't rise until later than planned?

4. What if interest rates go up? Or the vendor dies before the deal is complete? Or they go bankrupt?

5. Is it really that easy?

Lease options explained

A lease option is an all-encompassing term. First, there is a long lease (three to seven years) and then there is an option to buy the property. You can use this to 'buy' a property for your portfolio or to 'sell' to a tenant buyer. A lease option is a way to take control of a property and its cashflow without having to take out a mortgage right now, but giving you the option of buying the property in the future at a price agreed today.

Let's start with the lease. A lease is a legal contract, which in this context is similar to an Assured Shorthold Tenancy (AST) in that it is a contract between two parties where one grants the other permission to stay in a property under certain conditions in exchange for a fee. A lease might grant a three-year stay for a monthly fee (rent) with the potential to give 30 days' notice to leave by either party. OK, so that is an easy concept.

A purchase option is another component of the contract and this separate document states that if conditions are met, the property can be bought for the agreed (today) purchase price at any point between now and the fixed date in the future. It might give the right to extend that date.

So a lease option in the way we use the combined term means two contracts that give the holder the right to rent the property for a fixed period of time and the right, but not the obligation, to buy the property for a price agreed today, but complete at a time agreed in the future.

So the advantages are that you control a house without having to have a mortgage – great idea if you have poor credit rating or no cash to invest... or is it? My experience of spending six months and £4,000 advertising for deals and coaching many other investors is that lease options are not as simple as many experts would have you believe. I also believe that the focus of the strategy is all wrong – out of balance. Let's go through it chronologically and you can form your opinion. As a caveat, I think you should definitely understand this strategy and use it if a deal is worth it but, personally, I do not think this makes sense as a sole and primary strategy in this market.

The focus of any strategy...

It has to be the cashflow. That for me is number one. If there is no significant cashflow, then there is no deal to be had. Why? Each deal comes with debt. All right, in this example the debt is held by someone else, but there is a debt to be paid on the property regardless.

Once I know a deal will cashflow according to my rules (and I will run through those in a minute), then I want to know how 'easy' the deal is to arrange. I believe that with increasing complexity comes increased time costs and increased risk.

Time costs refer to how long it will take compared to other strategies to get a deal to the stage where it generates income. I call this return on time invested (ROTI) (see Chapter 17).

The other aspect is risk – the risk that I invest my time and energy and a deal does not complete. Now that risk is ever present, in traditional buy-to-let as well as lease options. I believe the risk that a deal will not complete is greater in a lease option.

Again, this can be explained easily. Think about the types of vendors we might come across in the course of an investment deal; homeowner moving as part of the normal course of life, repossession organisations, probates, estate agents and solicitors. These are all 'normal' players in the buying and selling game.

Targeting vulnerable and distressed vendors

One of the primary flaws in the lease option strategy is that it requires you to target vulnerable and emotionally distressed vendors. Some people call these people desperate sellers or motivated sellers. The truth is they are in some sort of mess and need help. I think you can already see why this strategy would be attracting attention from the FSA and others.

This means that in the course of negotiating the 'sale' or lease option of the property from the distressed and emotionally vulnerable seller, you will adopt some of that stress in order to get the deal done.

A lease option deal will definitely take more of your time to reach completion than a straight purchase from an estate agent. Therefore, when I did a time cost comparison I worked out that I could source more deals in one year compared to potential cashflow and capital gain from one lease option!

Let me explain (and trust me on the numbers): I could source one property deal per month for a fee of £5,000 each, totalling an income of £60,000. How many lease options would you need to complete on to get this sort of income? Your only source of income is the rent surplus. Any cash given by a tenant buyer (the golden goose that everyone hunts for) is their money, their deposit. On top of this, you will have the costs to arrange, possibly as much as £4,000 in solicitor fees AND the cost to refurbish the property to a rentable state. Unless of course you hunt for the other golden goose... the tenant buyer with trade skills who is prepared to move into a property in a mess and do it up while paying your rent. Was that very cynical sounding? Sorry, it just comes from experience and over three years on the forums listening to these deals!

I have even posed questions asking people to explain or name a deal they have completed on... need I finish the sentence?

If the vendor was not in distress, they would sell through an estate agent in the traditional way – so you are going to be explaining a new method of 'not-selling' your home to someone who just wants to get rid of the source of their stress.

If you are truly interested in win-win-win solutions, then great – please help people because there are vendors in a mess. However, take on the property deal in the full knowledge of what you are taking on.

The reality of the process

I discuss this strategy at length in my second book *Make More Money from Property: From investor thinking to a business mindset*, when I talk about return on time. The example I give is of a mentee who had been working a lease option strategy for a year and only closed one deal worth £200 per month. That was a lot of work for a low return.

Don't get me wrong, if you do this alongside a job, then you are definitely on your way to early retirement.

In my experience, if you know how to find buy-to-let properties that provide a great cashflow, then why not set up a business doing just that?

You still need rules to make a lease option a safe strategy. These include an exit strategy for the deal, profit margins, what happens if interest rates go up, the vendor dies before the end of the term or worse goes bankrupt – have you planned for these contingencies?

More details

A purchase option will involve agreement of an 'upfront payment' (similar to the deposit concept in a normal purchase). Then monthly payments over a number of years, like normal mortgage payments. Finally, at the end of an agreed time, you can purchase the property at a figure that was agreed at the beginning of the contract.

The upfront payment can be as little as £1 if you are negotiating to 'buy' a property using an option, and as much as 5% of the 'purchase' if you are negotiating to sell an option to someone else. In a sense, a lease option is very much like buying a car on lease; you would put down an initial deposit (or maybe trade in your car for a set value) and then make monthly payments.

At the end of the agreed term, you would have the choice to either buy the car for a pre-agreed figure or hand the car back. A lease option on a property is very similar to this.

So to summarise, there are two key parts to the lease option strategy:

1. You could lease the property from a home owner and gain permission to lease the property (i.e. rent it) to another tenant. In effect, you are acting like a letting agent with maintenance responsibilities, but with rights to all the profit from the rent (after the cost of the vendor's mortgage, insurance and repairs). Have you budgeted for the repairs?

2. The other part to the option (and the cherry on the cake) is agreeing a purchase price with the vendor today, with a delayed finalisation of the deal. In effect, you are agreeing the price and the option to buy, but you are not obligated to buy as you would be with an exchange of contracts.

Let's get into the detail now

There are lots of numbers and terms involved, and there are four main figures that you need to consider and negotiate when either entering into or selling an option. Let's make things easier and simply talk about how you can use an option to take control and eventually buy a property. Do remember that this is only one example and options are a useful tool in the professional investor's armoury.

1 Purchase price

One of the most challenging things to consider is the purchase price of the property. As with all deals, you need to know that you are paying a fair price for the property. What is a fair market value?

When you negotiate a traditional buy-to-let purchase, your aim is to buy in equity at the point of purchase, i.e. when you complete on the mortgage, because that is when you are setting the level of the debt. If you agree a price of £100,000, then your debt will be a percentage of that (the LTV you have borrowed) and you will have to pay it back.

So, with a lease option you are effectively agreeing a purchase price sometime in the future. What you are saying to a vendor is that you will agree to buy their house today for £100,000, but you will pay them in three, five or 15 years – you choose.

In the meantime, you will (effectively) pay their mortgage and take on responsibility to repair and maintain their home. This means that the vendor can move out of the property and move on with their lives, without the financial cost of the property hanging around their necks.

When you negotiate the 'purchase price' you can take the view that you can afford to agree a price close to the asking price because when you finally complete on the deal in, say, three, five or seven years' time, the real value of the property will have increased and you will be buying below future market value.

Circumstances and the homeowner's need to move will impact on their likelihood of agreeing to a current market value purchase price with delayed completion. It depends on the depth of rapport you build with the current homeowner and what they want or need to move out of the property.

2 Timescales or the term of the lease

When negotiating the lease you also ask for the option to buy the house at an agreed time in the future. You are effectively agreeing the future purchase price now. So, if you are buying a house using an option, it would be a great idea if you could agree to buy the house at today's price and then actually only pay for the house when it has increased in value (thereby gaining the equity we normally look for when buying in the traditional way).

When thinking about the 'term' of the lease you will need an understanding of the property market in your area and for your specific property. If prices are moving well and increasing, then you could agree a shorter time. If prices are moving more slowly or declining, then you might want to agree a longer lease so that you give house prices a chance to recorrect and increase before you are required to complete on the purchase part of the option.

The length or term of the option to buy will be determined in some ways by the price. What you want to achieve is a term for the option that is long enough for the house to increase in value so you can complete, using for example a 75% mortgage, which would cover the full purchase price.

If you agree to buy a house for today's price of £70,000, you need to calculate when you think the property will be worth £100,000. What do you think? Three years? Seven years? Longer? It's quite tricky. That's why you also need to ensure that you have the right to extend the term of the contract in case house prices do not climb as quickly as you thought. The main principle here is to agree as long a term as possible, and then buy sooner if it suits you.

3 The upfront payment (deposit)

An 'upfront payment' can be as low as £1 or it can be enough money to pay the homeowner's rent and deposit on a new property, their removal costs or some other financial cost that they are worried about and need to pay, if you are really coming from a win-win-win position.

This initial payment is totally negotiable and really starts at the point where you understand what the homeowner wants to achieve from their business dealings with you. If they want to move out, that is exactly what you want to achieve as well. Now what needs to happen? Do they need money to move? If not, then do not feel obliged to offer a large upfront payment.

Alternatively, if equity and their circumstances allow, you could help them get an equity release from the property and use that as a deposit for their next property.

When looking to sell an option to a tenant buyer you would calculate the upfront payment to either cover your expenses in negotiating the deal or even supply the funds to give to the homeowner. Your overall aim is to agree a contract to lease a property with an option to buy it at some point in the future for as little initial outlay as possible. Remember to factor in repair costs to get the property rentable and the solicitor's fees for you and the lease-option grantor!

4 Monthly payments

In most instances, monthly payments are simply the cost of the mortgage payments. Sometimes you come across homeowners who have second loans.

The principle thing to remember is that the potential rent you will get once the property is let out must cover the cost of the mortgage payments now and in the future when interest rates go up.

At this stage things could get complicated. You will need to be good at maths and understand this strategy fully. Make sure that you learn lease options the English way, as our rules and mortgage conditions must be met upfront. The other point to make is the importance of an expert team to support you! If you can control the property for the length of the agreement, you are in the best position to rent the property. The difference between the rent and the mortgage is your profit.

Who agrees to a lease option?

As I explained earlier, the homeowner is more likely to be in some form of distress. They could also be landlords who might want to have their property let on a long-term basis without the cost of management fees. A landlord might be happy to relieve himself of the responsibility of the property. And, of course, vendors who can't sell their houses for a number of reasons may be interested in this approach. There is another strategy called 'rent to rent' (see Chapter 15) that is much easier and less controversial than a lease option.

Every situation will be different as it depends on the vendor's previous experience, what they want the end result to be and in what timescale. Geographically, this strategy has different results across the country. This strategy can take time, but once the vendor understands that you have a good legal team in place and a solid contract, they can become more comfortable with the situation.

Whatever situation the vendor is in, they are likely to be more vulnerable and with that comes a professional duty of care. It is your responsibility to be sure that the deal will work for you over the period of the agreement. While you might not have a legal obligation to buy the property, I believe you have a moral obligation to make the payments you agree to – not just do it for a while until it gets difficult and then pull out!

Tenant buyers – the other side of the equation

Putting a tenant buyer into the property, especially someone who is willing to do some work on the property (the golden goose with knobs on), can ensure the property is looked after, as the tenant buyer will treat and maintain the property as if it was their own. This also means that there is regular (almost) guaranteed cashflow coming in.

A tenant buyer is the world's best tenant, and your best asset, as they are not moving into a house, they are moving into their home. The tenant doesn't view the property as a normal rental property. They move in and spend their own money adding value to the property. The tenant builds an emotional attachment to the property. You will need to maintain your relationship with them as they are, in effect, your most valuable asset. After all, you don't own the house.

Like any business, property investors can always get themselves a bad name if they want to. The principal of this strategy is building a relationship with people who are in a difficult situation. They want to move home for some reason and can't. You can help. Build that relationship and find a mutually acceptable way forward.

Think of the vendor; don't aim to back them into a corner – keep all the options open. Whatever you do, do it with the vendor's interests in mind. If you put a marketing plan together, you might be able to find vendors in this situation. Remember that, above all, have a good legal team behind you, as it is important to get things right from the start.

To summarise...

Understand how the strategy works, understand the numbers involved and create your own set of lease-option buying rules. These should include:

- Area and exit strategy.
- Payments, rent and mortgage costs – what's the profit and will it stand an increase in interest (build that into the contract)?
- Flexibility – what if prices go up sooner or, worse, not quickly enough?

- Vendor consequences – what if they die or go bankrupt, or never come back?
- Vendor consequences – what if they do come back? Have you been fair? Consider a profit share – remember win-win-win.
- Does the time work for you – consider your time investment. Is this a good use of your time?
- Remember the costs involved – marketing upfront, refurbishing the properties to rent, your solicitor, broker fees.
- No matter what they tell you, a lease option is not an asset. The only asset in the deal is your tenant who pays the rent and makes the profit – you are a letting agent!
- No matter what they tell you, selling a lease-option contract to another (foolish) investor is just what the banks did when they sold derivatives of bad debt – there is no asset to sell.

In my experience, if you know how to find a deal in a cashflowing area, then simply find people willing to invest – they have a different mindset and marginally less emotional issues to deal with. You will make as much, if not more, money for less stress.

Chapter 13

Assisted sales

In the first edition, I spoke about assisted sales as being a great cash generating strategy. Effectively, the strategy is to help a vendor to sell, as opposed to sourcing which is helping an investor to buy.

During the last couple of years, horror stories of vendors being emotionally devastated by the deals they agreed to have started to float around.

Let's start this whole section by repeating that being an ethical investor is the only way to be. If you don't feel that way, then I guess you would also have stopped reading several chapters back anyway!

We only need a relatively small amount of income to be financially free – for most people £2,000–£3,000 is enough to cover their costs. Double that and you will have a great cashflowing strategy and contingency. If you remember this, then there is no need for you to rush, struggle or bully people. Enough preaching, let's get into the detail.

Assisted sales explained

You might start by attracting private sellers through your marketing. Their situation may mean that the deal does not work for you as the buyer of discounted property. You will have an arsenal of strategies including lease options and assisted sales as a way to help. Offering a lease option makes you a letting agent. Doing an assisted sale can make you an estate agent.

If the latter is the case, then I feel personally that you deserve a fee for your time, like an estate agent. I struggle to see how acting like the 'House Doctor' shown on the television means you are entitled to 50% or more of someone's equity from their home, regardless of the financial trouble they were in!

To me, the real idea of the assisted sales strategy is that on your travels you will come across deals that do not work for you as an investor. However, the vendor still wants to sell and you could use your knowledge to help them. The turning point of this strategy is that the property will be a private sale and not already on the market with an estate agent and you will recognise how you could add value to the deal in order to maximise the final sale value. This is way beyond the role of an estate agent – this is a property entrepreneur. You might even use some of your cash to enhance the property through development, an extension or splitting titles.

In some cases, the fees charged have been £10,000s of pounds. A disproportionate fee for the work involved as a house doctor, but a fair profit share to off-set the risk of using your personal cash! There are stories that some vendors have been so emotionally depressed as a result of this type of agreement, made while they were stressed and vulnerable, that they have harmed themselves! Really, is that how you want to do business?

So, if you find a suitable assisted sales property, what might it look like? Well, it could be a large two-bedroom house that you could reconfigure. It could be a house where there is scope for a loft or rear extension. It could be a large property split into flats, but not under separate titles. It could be owned by an investor and they might be struggling or over leveraged... It could be anything where you with your expert knowledge could add significant value for relatively low outlay.

This, like lease options, is a secondary strategy in my opinion. Beware – when a deal does not work for you as a traditional investment deal – question yourself as to whether you have time and experience to pull off an assisted sale and then make your choice. Personally, I would consider offering a fee for my time if I was simply selling, or a profit share if my cash and time added significant value. If making a profit share agreement, personally I would agree a split of 40/60 or even 30/70 in favour of the vendor – it is, after all, their home and their inheritance.

Case study

To assist, split, option or have an adventure?

I have been working with a mentee who has architectural skills and they found a deal that they knew they could add value to.

The property was a probate and in a desirable area. It needed refurbishing but it could also be enhanced from a two-bedroom property to a four-bedroom.

My mentee built a relationship with the vendor, through the estate agent, to the point where the vendor was prepared to accept an offer. Outline plans were drawn, quotes for the renovation and refurbishment project were received and we started to run the numbers for a couple of strategies to fund the deal.

Our options were:

- A lease option to secure the deal and agree the price – not a bad idea as it would secure the deal and, yes, agree the future price. However, we wanted to be clear that our aim was to buy and sell and not get confused with renting, so in fact we just needed an option or a lock out agreement.
- Assisted sale – well, yes, we could assist the vendor to achieve a higher valuation but, in this case, the sale was a probate which would mean that the higher end value would create higher inheritance tax liability. There was also an estate agent in the chain of contacts. So, a conversation was held to get them to waive the first set of fees in return for higher end fees when we sold at the new sale price. The danger here was if we couldn't find a buyer.
- To buy outright with commercial funding, bridging or a mortgage with no redemption penalty and low fees. The disadvantage of this strategy was that it required a lot more cash input, but it meant that the deal was definitely secure and, with a solid database of investors, I could see a secure win-win for everyone involved.

The property

The property was a 1960s two-bedroom split-level house sitting high on a city hillside with stunning views of a cathedral – a much sought after location for those wanting close, easy city access yet stylish seclusion for their home life. This was checked with local estate agents to assess the potential redevelopment value and most importantly demand.

The property was well maintained though dated and ideal for renovation. The layout consisted of a huge open-plan lounge/dining area, with panoramic views on three sides, which led into a large kitchen. There were two bedrooms to the rear with a separate bathroom. At the lower ground level, there was a large double garage plus a workshop.

The house was originally marketed at £320,000. There was a significant amount of work to be carried out for an ordinary purchaser. The estate agent was happy for my mentee to deal direct with the vendor (his fee was of course guaranteed no matter what). This spoke of a high level of trust and relationship, which is critical with such a key member of the deal team.

After much negotiation, an initial purchase price of £260,000 was agreed. This was still above the stamp duty threshold – another tax to contend with – so more negotiations were entered into to agree a purchase price and a fee component for allowing a potential delayed completion.

Building regs, trees and the rules!

No permissions were required for the redevelopment, just a Building Regulations application, which the mentee could handle directly. Tree preservation orders were checked as the Local Authority was keen to keep trees lining the road frontage – they agreed for them to be trimmed. It is always important to keep on the right side of the authorities.

The road on which this property lies has uniquely designed properties, all individual and therefore difficult to find comparisons for the figures involved. This was to be a challenge throughout the process – but when sold to a member of the general public as their home, emotions will take over!

Options for development

First, the garage and workshop could be converted into two additional bedrooms with either an ensuite each or a shared bathroom. This level would be accessed via a new spiral or standard staircase from the current main living space above. This would create a four-bedroom property and would require the lower level walls to be tanked, floors insulated and windows inserted in place of the garage doors.

A second approach would be to utilise the roof space – a traditionally constructed roof rather than trusses, which makes alterations easier – to create two new bedrooms with ensuite or a shared bathroom with a new staircase from the existing living area. There was ample space as the rooms were large. The lower floor garage could stay in use and the workshop could become a games room.

The exit strategy

The selling agents were confident of a resale price, once the works were complete, of between £370,000 and £400,000. They had previously had a prospective purchaser for the exact property who had £420,000 to spend and would have bought it had it been in an updated state where he could have moved straight in without having to undertake the works himself. The local builder and a former resident both firmly believed the asking price was much higher at £450,000 due to the location and the view.

A critical factor in the success in selling this unique deal was the mentee's contacts, they were well connected in circles where potential buyers were likely to come from, for example, the armed forces, business executives and other wealthy individuals. It is vital to know that you are creating a product that you can sell.

We created an ideal scenario which was to market the property as the refurbishment works commenced, having already entered into a lock out agreement with the vendor. When the buyer was identified they could then influence the final touches to their own taste and colours, thus providing a unique personal service tailored to their individual requirements.

This became the start of a complete brand – a personalised development service for those who want a quality home but without the hassle of making a house their home. We can make any house your home! The service includes sourcing the property, surveying and planning alterations, dealing with and submitting applications to the relevant local authorities, arranging and overseeing the building and refurbishment works and handing over to the new purchaser.

In the end, the deal worked as follows:

- Initial purchase: price £250,000.
- Fee to vendor for delayed completion: £10,000.
- Building budget, including contingency and overrun: £62,000.
- Cost of borrowing on initial purchase price, including fees (£187,500 @ 5.5% for 6 months): £7,500.
- Cost of borrowing deposit and costs from investor partners – repaid through profit share.
- Resale value: £410,000 (less agent and solicitor fees £7,500).
- Fee for project management: £23,000.
- Total cost to buy and renovate: £360,000.
- Profit to investors: £50,000. Based on £150,000 borrowed to allow overrun (£132,000 budget).

A definite example of using investor and entrepreneurial thinking to create more for everyone.

Chapter 14

Adverse possession

We all know there are thousands and thousands of empty homes. It is both criminal that properties are left to rot while people are homeless, and equally mind boggling that the owners would allow them to rot. One thing's for certain, we will never understand what goes on in other people's minds – we can only guess (and even then I bet we would still be wrong half the time)!

There are two possible routes that you could take when faced with this dilemma-cum-opportunity:

- Contact and develop a relationship with the local council, even apply for grants and start the long process of renovating our country one house at a time.
- Identify an empty property, stick a notice on the door and when no one comes to complain or remove the sign, then you get a locksmith and break in! You then proceed to rent this property out benefiting from the income. A squatting landlord if you like (and I don't like) and then steal the property in 10-12 years if no one notices!

Was that second option a bit harsh or loaded? The frightening fact is that people are running courses on this second strategy. I am both intrigued and horrified in equal measures. One half of me says that just because there is an ancient law (started by William the Conqueror to control land and therefore his power) doesn't make it right. The other entrepreneurial half of me will admit that here is a massive opportunity.

I think my personal dilemma, as with the aforementioned assisted sale, questions where is the win-win for the original owner? If the original owner has truly vanished or died without heir, then why should I benefit over everyone else? Maybe I do have the skills and the talent to spot these empty properties…. As I read about such strategies, like lease options, BMV, NMD and even assisted sales, the marketing material seems to say 'use me as a quick way to get rich' (even if it sails close to the legal wind or is at someone else's expense).

I asked myself whether I am limited by a belief that all money and profit has to be as a result of hard work? And, honestly, the answer is no! In my second book, *Make More Money from Property: From investor thinking to a business mindset*, I describe a business strategy (sourcing) which I know is easy once the system is in place. In fact, I argue that once you find what works, focus on it and do it again and again!

Perhaps what is not explained is that, apart from the moral issues I alluded to in my loaded introduction, there are costs and risks.

The process involves:

- locating these properties
- researching ownership, which takes time and money. You need to see if you can find a vendor, otherwise you are wasting your time in taking an adverse possession. Once your notice is posted an owner may emerge. What is your strategy to handle this? What costs will you already have incurred?
- locksmith costs to seize possession and change the locks – are you aware of what constitutes break and entering and what is adverse possession?
- restoring water, electricity and gas connections. If the property has been empty for some time, then the services are likely to be off and the property in disrepair – you need to budget for this.
- risk – the owner could return at any time. You are not on the title deeds, so what gives you the right to rent the property to another person?

I am sure that trainers of this strategy have all the answers. Personally, and I am sure you have guessed, I cannot see this as ethical or even sensible. It is easy to see how this works on empty parcels of land. The costs are minimal – just fencing, signs and a gate to declare it as your possession. What of the property that needs £5,000 or £15,000 of work to bring it to standard, and that is on top of the costs of researching ownership and tracking a registered owner? If you worked in partnership with the council, you could attract grants and support. You could have no headaches. Of course, you would have a mortgage (if you can get one) and that appears to be part of the attraction. Money for nothing.

I invest in the north and the volume of empty homes is staggering. I also know their internal condition! I still feel that if a property is truly empty and without a rightful owner, then the State should acquire, renovate and rehouse our most vulnerable members of society. I still feel uncomfortable that one single individual would benefit over everyone else. Maybe I just need to grow up and get real. If this strategy works for you and you don't feel the same as me, then I wish you every success.

No doubt in another few months you will hear of people selling adversely possessed properties to other so-called investors – another derivative of thin air! I just find this all very odd. If you feel comfortable, then please make sure you get thoroughly trained. Work out who is doing it, ask for live examples, ask for examples of what can go wrong and, again, live examples. Anyone who is really pursuing this strategy must have made mistakes – get them to talk about them. If you're still comfortable, then go ahead and very best wishes to you.

Chapter 15

Rent to rent

At last, a strategy that makes sense. In its most basic form, this strategy is a form of sub-letting. Contrary to popular belief, it is not illegal. Some letting agents use a special 'Corporate Let' contract, while others have adopted this strategy themselves. There are a number of legal and other issues you must adhere to, to avoid major pitfalls, such as correctly worded ASTs, ensuring the primary landlord is on the mortgage correctly and that there are insurance products in place. And, above all, making sure that you have an exit strategy – what happens when you want to hand the property back? This strategy helps others and enables you to benefit in the meantime – win-win! So what do you need to do?

- Find a landlord who is old, tired, bored or a long distance away and offer to help.
- Agree a contract to rent their property.
- Identify a strategy to maximise the rental income and you keep the profit.

In a sensible world, you would be looking to multi-let or enhance an HMO. You will again need to be aware of costs upfront and legislation. Unlike lease options, you will save on expensive solicitor fees and significant refurbishment costs (although there will be some needed).

Unlike an adverse possession, you are working in partnership with the current owner, often via a letting agent to benefit you both. And, like the best type of assisted sale, you get paid to enhance a property for the mutual benefit of all parties.

In the long run, you might find that the original landlord does agree to sell – that may be a bonus. The downside is that you will be a letting agent. However, imagine if you could find these deals in your area – that would be mightily convenient.

I worked with a coaching client who effectively operated this strategy by luck rather than judgement. They knew an investor who lived a long way from a small bundle of properties. They effectively acted as a letting agent. The landlord and investor agreed a profit level that the landlord wanted – it was then up to the investor to maximise the rental income and benefit from any remaining profit.

Be careful as with all deals to make sure that it stacks up for you. What resource does a deal need? Your time, which is finite and valuable? Your knowledge, which is abundant and a replenishable resource to be leveraged? Or your money, which again I would suggest is finite and valuable but can also be leveraged? Then decide on the value of using or risking those resources and make sure you charge or earn accordingly. I hope this makes sense. Think what the consequential or potential loss is and work out what compensation you want in return.

If it's not a lot of time and only requires some of your knowledge, then that might have a middle level value to me but a high value to someone else without the knowledge – so what value would you place on that? However, if a deal requires your time and money, then personally I would want a higher return for those resources as they have a high value to me if irretrievably lost – think about the potential consequences!

What if you could maximise the rental income by letting a property as an HMO or even a professional let, so that there was enough profit to pay someone else to be the letting agent – a perfectly sweet deal then!

Case study

Multi-let without the sweat (MLWTS)

As this strategy will effectively create a lettings business, you need to be clear about what works best for you in terms of area, property type and tenant type. Both LHA and student tenants can be quite demanding, so focusing on young professionals whom you 'train' to call your build team with problems will make this strategy a lot less time intensive!

My good friend, Francis Dolley, and his daughter Emily have made this strategy an art form and shared an example with me so you can see how the numbers work. They operate in Bristol and work with professional tenants.

Now, remember, you are essentially renting the property from a letting agent or landlord. So to acquire (let) an average property in Bristol would need the first month's rent and a deposit of £2,000. The letting agent fees are around £400 and average refurbishment costs are £750.

'This is not a misprint!' said Francis. 'We are very particular with the properties we take on. We are able to keep refurb costs to a minimum, and we have also discovered a very cheap method to furnish them. This is essential as we do not own the property. We also put aside a contingency fund of £350 per property.'

So what are the pitfalls of this strategy?

People often ask, 'What if the primary landlord asks for the property back after the initial term?' Normally the 'tired' landlords who willingly agree to this type of strategy are feeing some pain – empty rooms, missing rent – and either don't seem to care or do not know what to do about it. This strategy is the answer to their prayers, offering them guaranteed rent with no voids and no hassle. In London, this place in the market is taken by the council and housing association schemes.

Francis and Emily found that most of their landlords live out of the area and are obviously only interested in receiving the monthly rent. Even if the landlord did take the property back after 12 months, you would still have made an excellent return on your investment. If the landlord terminated the agreement, you would of course remove all the items that made the property more desirable and you would no longer be managing the property, which would put the landlord right back where he started. Most landlords would be smart enough to recognise this.

As Francis commented, 'We have had only one landlord out of nine ask for their property back and this was due to illness. We always pay the rent on time, we look after the properties and we don't bother the landlord with constant problems. Why would they want to go back to empty rooms and unpaid rent?'

Emily added, 'You may not be able to rent the rooms. You must fully research your target area and tenants both on and offline. We have totally systemised this process. We had one underperforming property with a small and difficult room to let. We decided to drop the rent to well below market value to prevent voids and did not renew this contract.'

Another significant factor to consider is what happens if it all goes wrong? You have a commitment and a contract with your tenants?

Emily and Francis explained two worst case scenarios:

1. If the landlord is declared bankrupt and a repossession order is issued, the tenant (you) can apply to the courts to postpone the date for two months and then issue your tenants with notice to quit. The court may make a further postponement if you can arrange payments directly to the mortgage company. On the plus side, the landlord could well become a distressed seller, which could be an opportunity for you to purchase the property cheaply, although the mortgage company would be obliged to try and sell for the maximum value.

2. What if the landlord dies? The responsibilities of the landlord will be transferred to the new owner of the property. In the first instance, this will be the executor, and then it will be whoever the property is sold or transferred to. The bank accounts belonging to the deceased may be frozen. If this is the case, you should keep the money safe and forward it to the new landlord as soon as you get the details. Family members of the deceased landlord may try and convince you to pay rent to them, but it could be that they may not be legally entitled to it. The new owners may wish to sell the property fast, which, again, could be a great opportunity for you.

Article 4 – the legal bit

You will need to keep up to date with the constantly changing legislation, such as Article 4, or you will become unstuck very quickly. In the past, Article 4 Directions were issued by local councils in circumstances where specific control over development was required, primarily where the character of an area of acknowledged importance would be threatened. They were more commonly applied to conservation areas. Councils have now extended Article 4 in some cases to entire cities. Commentators have referred to this as the de-studentification of entire areas. This does not necessarily affect the MLWTS strategy if you follow some straightforward guidelines. You will need to check with your council to see if Article 4 has been implemented in your area.

What makes this a good strategy?

Well, personally, I think this strategy says what it does on the tin – it's simple and straightforward and a route to income – providing you can organise and plan it properly.

The main benefits of using this strategy are:

- it limits exposure to interest rates, as the lease fees are fixed, giving a reliable long-term cashflow
- it lets you integrate the management of your existing portfolio and gives you the economy of scale to grow your business
- a massive return on investment – Francis and family make on average £535 per property for an average of £3,500 cash input – that's 1834% ROI!
- it's fast – find a property, get it rented and get the cashflow – no delay for surveys, brokers or mortgage offers. Again, Francis' fastest deal was three days from initial viewing to cashflow!

Critical success factors:

- A targeted area with well-managed relationships with local letting agents.
- Clear strategy on property and tenant type.
- Highly organised with good systems and structures in place.
- Know the relevant legislation – you have committed to pay the landlord!!
- Reinvest the cashflow into buy-to-lets and HMOs of your own.

Chapter 16

Angel investors – stepping up a gear

In 2010, as part of my research for the first edition of this book, I was really lucky to have a lengthy conversation with Parmdeep Vadesha about angel investors and how and where to meet them.

Who are angels?

Angel investors are people who have access to significant amounts of cash and a desire to earn a reasonable rate of return on their money by investing in property (or businesses). They are not interested in doing any of the background work, such as finding the deal, negotiating, managing the builders and managing the property. They have the money and that's what they are bringing to the table. They expect you to do everything else in terms of finding the opportunities and putting the deal together – basically doing the legwork.

Angels could give their money via a bridging company, but they prefer a level of involvement directly in a project. They will also be making a better rate of return on their cash by lending it directly and not sharing the profit with the bridging company.

Your share of the business arrangement is that you have the skills and the knowledge to put deals together. You also know how to manage the properties and how to make sure that the deal is either sold or refinanced, so that the investor's money can be paid back with a good rate at the end of a fixed period.

The role of the angel

The role of the professional angel investor is as the provider of the money and to have a strategic view of the project. Your role is to make sure that things happen and get done on time. The investor will be looking to make sure that you will do whatever it takes within your means to make sure the property is completed on time, that the build teams turn up, the work is done and the project goes to plan. Then the investor will want to know that the property is presented for sale in the best possible way, and that you will manage the estate agent to push it until it gets sold.

So how does this differ from borrowing money from family and friends?

If you look at this from an overall prospective, there are several differences worth noting. First of all the 'terms' you will get from an angel investor will be different from the terms you would get from family members and friends, or even a member of the public who has the available cash.

The investor will be somebody who doesn't know you, so their terms may be stricter regarding when they would like their money paid back and what the penalties might be if it isn't paid back on time. They will be very business-like – investing is their business.

There is a definite downside to working with people who give you easy terms. It does not give you the same stringent level of discipline that you will get when constructing a deal with an unfamiliar investor, and an angel investor in particular. Working with people who have stricter guidelines builds good discipline and creates better deals.

Your proof is in the pudding

Private investors have to believe that you can do what you say you are going to do. If there is a specific deal that you have in mind, or something you have done in the past, tell them about it. Be proactive and email them. Attach pictures of deals you are looking at and talk about what you are doing. Then get them to come and have a look at some of the properties you are looking to buy. They can meet you, see the property and that's when the investment – in you – starts to take place.

For an experienced angel investor who has done deals before, all they really want to know is the ROI, the timescale, the amount of risk involved and the soundness of your plan.

The investor will want to know if you are the kind of person who can put that plan into action and make sure that deal gets finished on time and the property can be sold. They will be focused on the end result. They will want to know that you can find, buy, refurbish or develop a property and get it sold or remortgaged so that they can get their money back.

An experienced investor may ask questions such as 'What's your relationship like with local estate agents?' They want to know this to make sure that the estate agent will work with you to push and make sure that your property gets sold above other people's properties.

The exit strategy is the critical success factor in this type of finance strategy. How is the investor going to get their money back so they can invest it again? Professional investors, much more than family and friends, need to know that you have thought through all the aspects of the deal and can make sure that a sale happens quickly.

Be professional

Whatever it looks like, you will need a professional document that presents you as a business investment opportunity, discusses and justifies your strategy as a sound investment, and explains the returns that an investor could expect. In effect, a sound business plan for this specific deal and your overall strategy.

Developing a business plan and professional profile will help you to clarify your thinking as you work through the process of generating the content. This will make you more confident when talking to investors. When the document is professionally developed and produced, it will add to your credibility as a professional business owner.

You must make sure that what appears on the web is congruent with your written message – so no drunken Facebook pictures – everyone checks everyone out these days!

How to meet angels

Quite simply type 'angel investment meetings' into Google; you will get millions of hits. Narrow down your search local to where you live. If you live further away you may still choose to come to meetings in London, as that 'is where the money is!'

As you become a regular attendee and get to know the other people there, you can start to learn about what kind of investments they have made in the past. An investor who has never invested in property and who may be nervous, as they don't really understand what's going on, will be a totally different proposition to an investor who has made lots and lots of property deals in the past. You really have to consider the investor and the different ways that you need to approach them.

Negotiating the terms of private finance

The terms of any deal are crucial as they lay out how you will benefit from the transaction, whether you are talking about a lease option, a traditional sale or the terms of a finance agreement. You need a deal that will motivate you to focus on the project and see it through to a speedy conclusion.

There are several components to think about, for example, the investor's return on that deal. This means how much money/profit they would make for lending you the money and what the interest rate would be.

You will find that most professional angel investors are looking for between 1–2% a month on the money that they lend you. With interest rates so low at the moment and people really struggling to get a return on their money in the bank, don't be afraid to ask for less than that. Remember, there are people out there for whom 5% per annum would be a fantastic return on their money, as it is 10 times more than they are getting in the bank.

As with professional bridging finance there could also be entry fees, which essentially pay for the legal fees of the investor, so in effect you have to pay their legal fees on entry to get the deal put together. You will also have to pay your own legal fees. Exit fees sometimes occur but look to negotiate, as there is no point in paying someone a fee to give them their money back when they are already getting interest on the loan.

Structuring the deal

You will need to think about the structure of the deal and how you are planning to pay the interest on the money you have borrowed. This needs to be agreed upfront. Rolling the interest payments up into a lump sum that is paid at the end of the deal opposed to monthly payments means that you would have better cashflow during the term of the deal.

Work out and agree how the interest is to be charged – whether it is calculated and charged daily or monthly. If charged on a monthly basis, you will need to be aware that if the sale of the property is delayed by a day or two falling into the next month of the agreement, then interest will be charged for the whole month even though you have only gone over by one or two days. Alternatively, if interest is charged daily, then interest will be charged only for the extra days and not for the entire month.

No matter who you are borrowing the money from, if everything goes well, then people will make money and everyone will be happy. But do remember to look at the worst-case scenario. You do need to think about what would happen if the property took longer than anticipated to sell. You need to figure this out before you sign the contract, as that's when you have the most leverage to negotiate extra terms. Work it through so that you are very clear about what your liability would be.

Things to focus on

Investors need to get to know you, and to do that you have got to go to networking events. You also need to be visible on the property forums, have your own website and multiple consistent profiles across all platforms, and of course go to business angel networking meetings.

This is a different way of doing business compared to a bank. For this to work, the investors have got to get to know you and to trust you. When you are getting money from a bank, it doesn't matter whether or not they 'like' you, their decision-making process is based on scores and computers. You might not even go to the bank, as it can all be done over the phone and by completing paperwork online, so 'you', your personality, makes no difference. (Having said this, if you are dealing with a bank on a commercial basis as business to business, then they will be looking at your experience too.)

Working with private investors is completely different, you are much more likely to get money from someone, even if you are not the most experienced or the best property developer in the room, if they like you, get to know you and start to trust you. Liking is very important. If a private investor doesn't like you, they simply won't lend.

When meeting investors for the first time, don't go for the jugular and ask for the money upfront – the investor has got to be able to trust you. It takes time to build up that relationship. Building up a series of trusting relationships is probably one of the best investments of your time. One or two good investors can allow you to buy lots and lots of properties and become financially free in a short space of time.

Choosing the right investment partner for you

When you choose an investor, aim to work with someone who has been recommended or has worked with the group you are part of. Talk to people who have dealt with that individual, so that you can get a feel for that person's temperament and what they might be like as a business partner.

In summary, angel investors are often professional investors who repeatedly cycle their money in and out of deals – just like 'Dragon's Den' on the television. However, with current interest rates so low, they can also be new and less experienced in that field. Get to know the person you are about to deal with, get recommendations, take a bit of time to 'interview them' as much as they will be interviewing you.

Present yourself as the professional and experienced property investor that you are. Develop your business plan and professional profile, for extra clarity and confidence in your concept and deals. Then be totally clear about your facts and figures so that you can negotiate a deal that will make you money and, more importantly, motivate you to succeed.

In a recent conversation with a client, they were bemoaning a joint venture deal they had agreed. Because they did not understand the numbers, the 'man with the money' was only earning 6% and they were earning under £1,500 for a whole year's work. A poor deal for everyone – not something an angel investor would agree to.

Make sure you understand the numbers for the investor and for yourself – if it's not a good deal, then it's not a good deal!

Chapter 17

Sourcing for cash – build a business

The final section of my second book, *Make More Money from Property: From investor thinking to a business mindset*, is on precisely this topic, but in much more detail.

In summary, the principle here is to build your business marketing funnel to such a degree that any spare leads that you generate and can't use for yourself can simply be sold on to someone else. Now comes the tricky bit. How? This is such a broad topic with so many variations I will have to break them down.

Lead-driven *vs.* client-driven approaches

When I talk about lead-driven sourcing I am talking about high numbers of leads generated through internet campaigns or leaflets, even newspaper adverts (if you are lucky). The medium doesn't matter; the concept is at one extreme – that you, the sourcer or lead seller, are collecting lots of people's names and contact details. You then sell them to a wide audience – you don't necessarily talk to the seller and don't know the investor. If you get your system right, you can 'pre-qualify' them into your database.

The other approach is where you source or find deals to meet the specific needs of a client or group of clients. This is like shopping to order and is a lower volume and more personal service. Let's look at the details and then talk about the strategies behind them.

Selling leads

All this requires is for you to establish a system where you attract a lot of leads and the most common approaches are internet sites, leaflet campaigns and newspaper adverts. In this model, you sell the 'cold' lead to another investor for anything between £25–£100. This is a high-volume business with a certain level of overheads depending on your internet marketing skills. I believe there is a growing distrust of this approach after many cases of databases being sold repeatedly, so be cautious.

The other simple challenge that few people promoting this idea actually discuss, is that a website is only a valuable resource if it is searched and for that to happen you need to be on the front page of Google – a tiny yet critical step that definitely requires high internet skills or the money to pay someone who can deliver a 'page one ranking'.

Packaged deals

In this case, you will have agreed a sale price with the vendor. Typically, people who sell packaged deals will work with a broker or financial advisor to create a no or low money down way of buying the lead. Now the price charged is closer to £3,000, which may include fees to the broker.

I have already voiced my opinion about this type of deal. Again, be cautious, as if you offer a system that involves mortgage fraud you could be at risk of a prison term!

Sourcing

An armchair service. This is all about relationships: first with the investor, to understand why they want to invest and then purposefully going out to source specific deals to meet their needs; and then with the vendors as you maintain contact with them to ensure the completion of the transaction. Now you are being paid anywhere between £3,000–£10,000, and the service you are offering may take your client to the point of purchase or all the way through refurbishment to the signing of the AST.

Fees are usually paid upfront for leads and on completion for deals and sourcing services.

Picking the right strategy

The right sourcing strategy will depend on your personal investment strategy. If you are happy to buy anywhere in the country, then you will most likely be looking for or generating leads from anywhere in the country. This forms the basis of your business.

Alternatively, if you have a specific niche – like HMOs in one location or cashflowing properties in the north – then your marketing will focus on and generate those specific leads. You could still sell these as cold leads. However, the added value comes when you really specialise and have your own local team. Now you can offer a packaged service and charge a fee by sharing business with your team and leveraging your fee.

Making it work in your favour

I believe that if you understand the principles of what makes an investment a great investment (i.e. cashflow and potential capital growth) and how to manage the process, then this business model can easily generate the cashflow that enables you to invest in property using other people's money. How you might ask? It is all about leverage. Whether or not you can afford to buy right now doesn't factor into this strategy. You are simply building relationships with estate agents or running your marketing campaign to attract deals. The only extra factor needed is the outlet for the 'spare' deals. The volume of spare deals depends on whether you are actively buying and the size of your marketing funnel.

As you market to attract properties, you also market or locate the appropriate pool of investors who would want to buy your spare deals – networking perhaps. Then, you offer spare deals and the appropriate level of service to your list of warm investors and charge a fee.

The benefit of an armchair service

If you love property, then offer an armchair investment service – you will need to find deals that specifically match the investment method you are an expert in. Wherever you are based, the draw for investors is cash on cash return – what's the ROI?

A more bespoke service definitely takes more time but is, consequently, worth more as a service. Now you will really need to think about what you have to offer that makes people want your product/service. Think about how you are different, then go and find the investors who need your help.

Converting deals into houses

Now, in true Kiyosaki style, simply reinvest your fees into property.

I offer a bespoke service to busy people who recognise the benefit of property investment, but neither have the time nor the knowledge to invest on their own. They have either cash or equity available, and they want a good rate of return on their investment. I specialise in building cashflowing property portfolios in the north of England, which acts as a foundation to future investing or a patch for a poorly performing existing portfolio.

My business is all about service, adding value and a great ROI and return on time investment (ROTI). I charge for my time, knowledge and experience and then use those funds to invest in another property for myself. My model enables me to buy every sixth property for myself using other people's money. The best bit is that I am following the same strategy. Whether I am buying for myself or whether it is for a joint venture or a client, it's a great use of my time.

Over the last few years I have increased my small pool of clients' personal wealth by just over £1million in income and equity.

Return on time invested (ROTI)

The easiest example of ROTI is to ask the question: 'How much does this activity earn me in an hour?' It helps, of course, if you know two other figures. First, how much do you need to earn an hour to cover your costs? And, second, how many hours do you need to work in a time period, day/ week or month?

For example, to earn the equivalent of £30,000 a year (before tax) divide it by 10 to get a monthly figure of £3,000. I chose 10 months as a working period because I want 8 weeks of holidays, including bank holidays. Now think of the number of working days in a month – let's just pick 20. So, divide £3,000 per month by 20 days on average to get £150 per day.

So, if you worked 20 days per month for 10 months at an income rate of £150 per day, you would earn £30,000 per annum before tax.

Now look at this… £30,000 per annum is selling six leads at £25 per day – could you do that, or even half of that? It is helping six bespoke clients at £5,000 each to invest in a cashflowing refurbished property with a tenant in place – could you do that?

Another way to look at your time, and the return you make on it, is to think about income generating hours. How many income generating or billable hours can you commit per week? Let's say three hours. Now you have three hours to produce your weekly target of £750 income. What can you do to earn that money?

Using the concept of ROTI, you could decide to free up more time by buying in a cleaner at £8 per hour and a book keeper at £10 per hour, and then use those extra three to five hours a week to earn money at a higher rate than you pay out to staff.

It is crucial to understand this concept. When you know how much you need to earn to cover your bills and how you can earn it, you will have found the path to financial freedom and it's much easier to get there if you stay on the path! These are just concepts to help you understand the topic – you will need to factor in contingencies and the cost of running your business. Plus, of course, the fact that you would like to earn more than £30,000 per annum!

So, I will just briefly mention the topic of bills here. Work out what you need to earn to cover your expenses (not the lifestyle of your dreams), your reasonable costs now. By doing this exercise, you might also reduce those expenses as you realise the things you are paying for that you don't need. I saved £455 per month in insurance policies and private medical health care that no longer covered us.

You can download resources to help with this on www.TheSourcersApprentice. com and buy my 2nd book which covers this in more detail at www.MMMFP. com. Armed with this information and knowledge, you can amend my original figure of £30,000 per annum to a more accurate figure and then focus on the income-generating strategy to help you achieve financial freedom.

Return on investment (ROI)

This is a similar concept that looks at how much you earn from a particular strategy so that you can compare your options.

	Three-bedroom house	Five-bedroom HMO
Purchase price	£65,000	£250,000
Loan borrowed	£48,750	£175,000
Cash deposit	£16,250	£75,000
Monthly rent	£525	£1500

Table 1: a three-bedroom house on a 75% loan at 5% and a five-bedroom HMO on a 70% loan at 6% (approximate rates).

Based on the figures in Table 1, the HMO seems to produce more rent if completely full. Now consider some of the costs. In Table 2, I have included a management fee on both sides because whether you use a letting agent or your own time, there is still a cost!

	Three-bedroom house	Five-bedroom HMO
Purchase price	£65,000	£250,000
10% management fee	£52.50	£150
Cost of mortgage	£203.12	£875
Utility bills	Paid by tenant	Estimate £100
Net income per month	£269.38	£375

Table 2

So, even allowing for management fees and utility bills for the HMO, it is still producing more cashflow per month. Now let's look at the ROI. If you prefer, you can think of this as comparable to the interest rate if you left the money in the back – what is your return?

The formula is easy:

Net annual cashflow divided by total money invested.

In this case, I have just based it on the deposit required. However, in reality you should include all costs such as survey, broker fee, sourcing fee, etc.

Net ROI   19.76%   6.2%

In my portfolio I like to compare the cashflow, which is an absolute must on any deal I do, with the added detail of the ROI. So I would get my full investment back from the deal on the house within five years, but would wait just over 16 years to get my investment back on the HMO.

Now go one stage further and think more strategically about how you invest your money.

If you had £75,000 to invest, what would you do? Buy one HMO because they have good cashflow or buy four smaller three-bedroom properties up north?

4 x £16,250 = £65,000 (With some cash left for contingencies.)

The rent from one HMO would still be £375 after costs.

The collective rent from four houses would be £1,077.52! That's massive.

Rounding up

- I leverage my time and get the best income generation possible by knowing how much I want to earn, how I can earn it and what tasks I can outsource for a lower hourly rate.
- I use my knowledge and experience to help other cash-rich, time-poor investors build cashflowing property portfolios that offer not only great cashflow but also a great ROI, and charge a fee that is in line with my target rate.
- I leverage the fees I charge by reinvesting and buying more property into my own portfolio, which in turn produces cashflow.

If you are still reading, then you definitely can apply these principles to your business and create a cashflowing business that enables you to invest in property using other people's money.

Chapter 18

Social media – making friends and finding deals

Social media is a revolution in terms of marketing. By using the combined power of the internet and the recommendations of friends, this powerful tool will get your message out there and attract the right sort of people and clients to you. It builds on the psychology of trust and referrals and combines that with direct access to millions of potential customers – all you have to do is get the strategy right.

My experience suggests (and experts agree) that one thing is clear: you must be aware of how you present yourself and why you are presenting yourself to the world.

There is a huge difference between a Facebook[6] account that you just use to communicate with family and friends, share photos and news, and a profile used by someone for business purposes.

If you want to do both, then you need two separate accounts, or learn how to separate your profile into lists for friends or for business. Drunken pictures of you at a party will not promote the right impression. However, if you are in business to have lots of scuba-diving holidays or drive a fast car, then those images may be more relevant. And Facebook is just the tip of a giant iceberg of possibilities.

Just remember that what you post and, worse, what others post about you stays online!

Different formats for different purposes

Traditionally, a business created a website as a virtual shop or shop window to promote their product or business concept. This clearly had its purpose and it will back-up and reinforce any other marketing messages that you place out there. If your aim is to meet people such as angel investors, lead

---

6   Facebook is an online social network site that many investors use as a business tool providing sources of information, leads, news and self-promotion. You don't have to play games, you can use it as a business tool.

buyers or vendors, the question is: how will they know to go to your site to read about you?

OK, you could pay lots of money to a clever web guy to 'SEO' your site, or you could take a social media approach to marketing and create a 'blog', a Facebook account and go on the property forums for free. It's very easy to get lost in the technology when using internet marketing to attract contacts. Your focus needs to be on answering the following question: what things can you do to enable people to 'know you, like you and trust you'?

One of the best things you could do is to have a blog that talks about what you are doing, for example the fact that you have just been to view a property. Post pictures of that property on the site, and maybe a quick interview with an estate agent you spoke to and possibly some examples of adverts you put in the paper.

Creating blogging websites is so easy now, but if you find this beyond the range of your knowledge, then find a great website guy or a brilliant social media girl who understands social media and can help.

The main principle for you to understand is why you are on the web. Depending on what client group you want to attract, from angel investors to landlords, present yourself on Facebook, LinkedIn, Twitter and other sites in the same professional and friendly way you would if you were meeting people in person.

Anywhere that provides a place where your client could go to learn more about you and what you are doing is perfect. It's all about having 'social proof '. This will give the investor or vendor confidence that you are someone who is capable of helping them to achieve their goals. You can also let people know that there are others out there who have either invested with you or have confidence in you, and are happy to work with you through the comments and connections that you make.

Focus on finding people who have a passion for property using the social networking sites. You could set up a group for people in your area. Look at which forums you should contribute to and get involved in discussions. You will attract clients.

It is definitely worth spending time to present yourself in all of these arenas.

The face-to-face side of marketing and self-promotion

While online social media easily exposes you to hundreds and thousands of contacts at the touch of a button, some people still enjoy the social aspect of face-to-face marketing. Social media now enhances and accelerates the process as people start to recognise you from your online presence, making it easier to approach you in person.

A great idea is to invite investors along to networking events that you attend. They will get to see you surrounded by people who like you, trust you and want to work with you. This is a fast-track way to increase their trust in you. In a short space of time it shows that you are the kind of person that other people like and want to work with.

Your investor or sourcing client will appreciate the fact that you are willing to introduce them to others and that says a lot about your confidence in yourself. That tells them that you are not insecure, that you are very happy in your standing and what you can do.

Make a commitment

There are some fantastic events out there and, as the marketing blurb would say, 'Find one near you now'. There really is no excuse not to get involved, even family commitments can be adjusted just for one night per month. To start, find one event, maybe through recommendation, that is near to you that you can attend and commit to regularly.

Make the commitment to attend three or four events in a row, if possible. Learn the culture and style of the group and get involved. Take your business cards with you. So many people still attend a networking event either without cards or with too few. The aim is to briefly get to know people in the room – mutually exchange details and then follow this up with a call or an email the next day.

Once you have the networking bug, spread your wings and join other face-to-face events, forums and groups online.

Take the initiative; contact people and say how much you enjoyed meeting them the night before. Ask if they have time to discuss an opportunity, or answer a question. No one minds – that's how relationships and potential joint ventures are formed. That is how I met everyone in this book and in the first edition.

Fantastic events

There are so many great events across the country now that there really is no excuse not to find at least one event per month. It is the quality of these events that prompted me to feature them in this second edition.

Remember that, depending on who you class as your target client, they may also be at other events, for example a gym social evening, a work do, a business networking forum. Wherever you are, talk to people – meet people – strike up conversations.

My approach to social media and networking

In late 2011, I finally managed to engage the services of a VA (a virtual assistant). This concept allows one person (the VA) to work for many and you, as a business owner, can employ them on an hourly basis in the knowledge that they have the skills, experience and loyalty of a full-time member of staff. There are so many ways to work virtually that you do not need to have someone travel to you to work with you – though I do still like the occasional visit.

Although I set up my own websites and I do all the blogging content, I use my technical team to do all of the difficult stuff that I can't even describe! They also help me to join all my various sites together and focus on the key word areas that I want to be known for. During the last few years, they have been a massive help. In 2012, with the launch of my second book, *Make More Money from Property: From investor thinking to a business mindset*, at a big do in central London, it was social media that spread the news and resulted in 85 people joining me to celebrate the book launch.

On the face-to-face side, I spend a lot of time networking at a specific selection of property events. It is quite easy to get carried away and be out every night of the week. I have picked a small number of local and high-profile events that both enable me to hear from great speakers and learn about the latest thinking in my industry, as well as network and raise my own profile as someone working successfully in property investment.

I do attend a business group hosted by Ecademy on a monthly and quarterly basis, as it provides both an opportunity to network in the true sense of the word and also to share business experience and expertise.

Growing your business team is a crucial part of your business development but it need not cost a fortune.

So top tips...

1. Create a blog – get help if you need it.

2. Create a presence on social media sites, but with a clear purpose – who are you and who do you want to attract?

3. Contribute to forums, set up groups and get involved online. If you just read, you will learn, but no one will know you were there unless you leave a comment. Beware, forums can become a time bandit!

4. Get business cards – it is so easy these days. Do I even need to mention the companies you can use?

5. Pick a networking event and commit. To download my presentation, '7 Top Tips for Making Networking Easier' go to www. TheSourcersApprentice.com

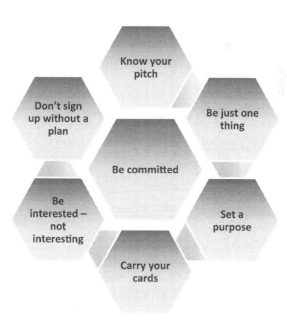

7 Top Tips for Making Networking Easier

6. Extension strategies once you get in your flow:

   - Start business networking – investors often own other businesses.
   - Make sure your blog leads to a site or an action that enables people to connect with you, for example join your newsletter, buy a product or services, make an appointment, etc.
   - Build a database. Whether you record your business cards in excel or on a database, start a list. Make a note of who they are, where you met them and why they are interesting. Back-up your list as your network is your net worth.

7. Come to the http://LondonPropertyConnection.com hosted by Deena Honey, Louise Wheeler and myself. Read more about it on page 150 – we are suggesting there is a different way to do property and an easier way to network…

Chapter 19

Protecting yourself and those with whom you are in business

Did you know that, in the UK, seven out of 10 people die intestate (without a valid will)? This means that important decisions on how their assets and possessions are distributed are left to the government to decide under intestacy rules. Many people assume that their spouse or partner will get everything if they die. Unfortunately, this is not necessarily the case. In fact, if you are not married or in a civil partnership, there is a good chance your partner will receive nothing.

This is going to seem like a strange chapter, but I feel that I need to include it. This topic came up quite early on in my personal journey and then really hit home in late 2010 when my best friend died, leaving her family to 'clear up' her property mess where she had made poor investment decisions through a 'property club'.

As this whole book is about using other people's money, some of those people will be family and friends; even the professionals will still have worked hard for their money in the first place. Even if you do have a will, how will your beneficiaries benefit from your estate? Will they have to sell the portfolio to raise money (some of which will be needed to pay death duties)?

Why not take out an insurance policy, place it in trust, include it in your will and then at least your family will have a guaranteed sum of cash to work with while they rearrange the finance of the portfolio? They could use the policy to clear the mortgages and keep the properties and the associated income (you could make that a rule in your will), or they could use the money to recruit a specialist to help them refinance the portfolio – think about it.

If you do already have a will, you need to ensure that it is still valid. For example, marrying or entering into a civil partnership after your will is made will normally revoke it. Alternatively, if you divorce or dissolve your civil partnership after your will is made, your will is not automatically cancelled.

Entering into a business arrangement or partnership may require changes. You need to read and check that your will is still valid.

I was amazed at how easy and inexpensive this process can be: my parents paid over £500 to go to a solicitor; we paid less than half for two wills. Life insurance, again, does not have to be expensive – unless of course you are old or smoke, or both. I had one partnership at the time of writing the first edition where we did not take out insurance. Therefore, at a time of serious illness, we had to get power of attorney to sell the property because we did not plan properly.

All my business partners have now written individual wills and taken out life insurance policies. I am now comfortable that anyone I borrow money from is protected but, more important than protecting my property investments, my family will also continue to benefit – which is, after all, part of the point (along with my holidays of course).

Bob and I are not married, but without him and his support I would not be able to focus and achieve my goals as easily or quickly – the business is as much his as it is mine. If you are in business with someone or have borrowed money from family or friends, then what provision have you made to repay that debt/loan?

Will your instructions be followed if you don't have a will?

Colin Griffiths very kindly let me reproduce a diagram from one of his leaflets explaining what would happen to your estate if you don't have a will. This can be found at www.TheSourcersApprentice.com. Take a look – is this what you want?

Epilogue

That's all for now folks – for a second time

In the Appendix, I summarise the key points that I have learnt about using other people's money over the last three years. I share with you what motivates me to keep going in the (sometimes) challenging property investment world, and finally let you know my plans going forward.

This final section of the book contains a series of comments from all the wonderful friends who have contributed to my business development through their fantastic property events. They are all professional and very successful investors, using different techniques and strategies. Some have developed associated property-related businesses; some use the services of others in their power team. All are generous, giving and supportive – great people to connect with. Make sure you work your way through all the events mentioned in the following sections of the Appendix, and more referred to on ThePropertyMermaid.com website.

Appendix

Lessons learned the hard way...

Seven and a half secrets to using other people's money to invest in property

My aim is to share the lessons I have learned about how to successfully invest in property with as many people as possible. I was a university lecturer and I can't let go of the belief that getting an education about a new business is vital to a person's success. I believe knowledge is the new money.

It seems obvious that if you could learn what other people are doing, find out how they did it and what mistakes they made, and then you could create your own even more successful approach.

I speak to so many people who got sucked in by potential 'get rich quick' schemes (I was almost one of them), people who have suffered, been stressed to the point of breaking and lost vast amounts of money. There are many more who started investing to have more time and are now working harder for less.

That's not what I am in business to do – I want to be even more successful and to leverage my money so that *it* works and *I* don't have to.

In the brilliant conversations I have with friends and fellow professional investors I remember so much, learn so much and make more explicit my own learning and understanding about the strategies and, of course, I learn new ideas and techniques. Talking to people and learning is crucial. Learn a strategy and then dissect it, unpack and take from it those parts that contribute towards your personal journey to financial freedom. Please let me know if I can help you in any way.

There are many more books to come – the next is waiting on my desk as we speak...

I do hope that you benefit from this 'sharing of my knowledge, lessons and mistakes' so that you can go on and create your own even more successful investment strategy. Then, when I write the third edition, perhaps you will appear in the Appendix sharing your story, knowledge and expertise.

First lesson – develop your personal investment plan

Understand why you are investing and what you want to get out of it. Understand how much your time is worth and how many hours – billable/chargeable hours – you need to complete each week to achieve that target.

This income will ultimately come from the properties that you invest in – along the way it will come from the effective use of your time in the right and time-cost effective strategies.

You will have challenges – if you don't, then you aren't doing enough! When those challenges arise, understanding the ultimate vision of your life will pull you through.

Scuba diving all the warm waters of the world is a metaphor for me. Yes, I want to do it too. It means a way of life, one not tied to a desk, freedom and choice being two of my core values. It means fun and adventure and learning new things along the way – more things that are important to me. It means time with my family and friends – without whom we would all be much lonelier!

The strategies and the business must support my life – so they are time effective, cashflowing in a hands-free way through the property portfolio. When I get bored of diving or just need to dry out, then I have a flexible business model that enables me to work when I choose to. I generate a great return on any of my time that I share with other people either through sourcing, mentoring or strategy sessions. This business generates additional income at a level that is worth my time. Not £2.50 an hour for a lease option.

My strategies support my desire for an easy, happy and stress-free life. They are not attracting distressed and emotional people into my life (well, not on a daily basis).

Pick your financial target, work out what your time is worth and then choose the right strategy for you and your future. Let me know if I can help, I definitely provoke the way people think about investing. Do you need a shake up or just a helping hand? If not me, who else can help you?

Second lesson – focus

Now you have your personal vision – an idea what you want life to be like – FOCUS on it!

Don't allow yourself to be distracted. Be laser-like in your vision and your actions. Yes, of course, still go to networking events – they are crucial. Yes, you will hear the other strategies that people are employing. Remember the amount of income you need. Relax.

With focus, you will achieve your goals. If you constantly flit from one strategy to another, like a poppy in the wind, you will get nowhere. Your journey will be like a ride at a not-so-fun funfair!

Focus

Follow one strategy, listen to others, take pieces of learning and build them into your overall plan and stay FOCUSED. What more can I say?

Third lesson – know the rules of the game and learn to leverage

From banks to mortgage lenders, credit card companies to angel investors, everyone is in business for a reason. Know what they want. Is it as simple as 'interest and charges' on the money they lend you, or will you be developing business relationships (as with angel investors – see Chapter 16) where the investor wants to 'know you and trust you' as well as lend you their money for a return?

The same applies to family and friends – you need to understand what they have been saving their money for and in what circumstances would they need their money back. Make sure that you have a plan to return it.

Managing and protecting your credit rating is all part of the same game. Learn how to play the credit card game (see Chapter 3). Learn how to build credit and improve your rating as well as protect your rating. This is an essential business skill that so many property investors still do not understand. Make sure that you are not one of them.

Learn to leverage and make money work for you – there is nothing wrong with that as long as you clearly understand the risks that come with the potential rewards.

Listen to people about the economy, read the right books, learn what caused the current problems and understand the radical solutions being suggested. I highly recommend *Bank to the Future: Protect Your Future Before Governments Go Bust* by Simon Dixon (Searching Finance Ltd, UK).

Fourth lesson – know what your market wants

Knowing your market and what they want is crucial to maximising your profit. So know:

- the difference between preparing a property for sale, as opposed to renting
- what your family member wants if they lend money to you
- how the terms of any money borrowed from a bridging company or an angel investor differ.

Tailor everything you do towards your target market – this means refurbishment, redevelopment, marketing and costs. Understand that your strategy and approach will make a considerable difference to the size of your profit margin.

Having said this, always have a second exit strategy in case the property market changes during the process of your refurbishment or redevelopment. Remember how quickly the market turned in 2007–2008 and how many people got caught out.

Make sure you are meeting the needs of your prospective buyer or tenant and not redecorating a 'home' according to your tastes! My tenants love laminate flooring and 'red' or 'blue' bedrooms for the football fans in the house. That's their choice – it's their home.

Fifth lesson – know the difference between a big portfolio and financial freedom

This is really the most important lesson. Lots of people can articulate how many houses they want (or have), some can tell you what cashflow they need to be financially free, but the crucial question is what will you do when you are financially free? You can all guess that I will be scuba diving until I am wrinkly or sucking the rust out of the oxygen tank. The key to success is visualising what your life will be like when you have all the income you need.

Then calculate this to a monthly cashflow target and work to that. I am so often asked, 'How many properties do you own?' What does that matter?

The questions should be:

- Do you have to work for cash anymore?
- How did you become financially free?
- Will you show me how?

My big 'why I invest in property' (apart from it makes so much financial sense) is that I want lots of holidays travelling the world and diving in all the warm waters I can find. I love taking underwater photographs. Bob and I share this passion and what nicer way to live life than to share a passion with someone you are passionate about? I really am very fortunate.

Of course that is just what my cashflow brings me – freedom and the choice to spend my time as I want. My long-term aim and why is to provide a financially independent future for my family and myself. I worked out how much income I needed in three levels: basic costs, contingency and business development. I then set about generating that income.

So what's more important – the size of your portfolio or the size of your rent cheque?

Sixth lesson – take responsibility for your financial future

I really started to explore this concept as I wrote my second book, *Make More Money from Property: From investor thinking to a business mindset*. I recognised consciously what I knew subconsciously – that the potential economic crises are backed-up waiting to burst into a brand-new day and that I needed to prepare myself and my family to become self-sufficient. In this interdependent world, one country's struggle is another country's recession!

I am already self-sufficient and, in my old age, I will pass on a large cashflowing portfolio to my children and grandchildren to provide for their future comfort and independence. I will take advice on the best way to do this but, in the meantime, I am insured.

What provisions are you making? What happens when you get old? Are you heading for an NHS nursing home where you will sit in a stinky chair rocking as you watch daytime television? Or will you own your own nursing home and have a penthouse (ground floor) luxury apartment waiting for you funded by your shrewd investment decisions.

I plan to slide into my grave shouting, 'Whoopee, what a ride!' Having lived a colourful, thick and full life as I travel my wavy line from cradle to grave, not a thin, straight, grey and white line of boredom and reliance on the government.

Seventh (and a half) lesson – take action

So you've read this book. Maybe you have done some training before; maybe you still have courses to do? That is great, but what action are you taking?

Get Clarity
in property investment

ROI

Financial Freedom

£££, not
# of houses

What's your plan – can I help?

- What is your financial strategy?
- Do you have the clear vision to understand where the money is in the deal?
- Have you calculated the numbers, your financial freedom target, the value of your time, your ROI rules?
- Do you have cash to invest or are you using other people's money?
- What is your investment model?
- Where are you going to invest?
- What will influence that decision? Do you have a job or are you doing this full time?
- What is your strategy and where will it work best?
- What is your business model?

Just stop making excuses and get on with it... Find an area and research it. If it works, great. If not, find another one. If you are confused by all the training, then get a copy of *Make More Money from Property: From investor thinking to a business mindset* and follow Section 3 step by step and get out there!

That's why it's only half a secret – because you really should know this by now!

Summary of the summary

The words that keep repeating are 'know', 'understand' and 'take action'. Maybe it's because I was a teacher that I hear and emphasise these words. Maybe you hear another message. I believe the most important thing is to learn from other people's mistakes – then avoid them and create even easier paths to financial freedom and success. That, of course, is why I wrote this book.

What motivates me through the tough times and the easy times?

As I rewrite this final section, I am in Sulawesi in Indonesia. Before writing the first edition, I had just spent an amazing three weeks travelling from Cape Town, then along the 'Garden Route' to Plettenberg Bay, and finally on to Durban.

I have said before that I was a university lecturer for a number of years and I loved that job. I never questioned what I learnt, how my boss treated me, the hours I put in. My pleasure and total satisfaction came from the role of sharing knowledge with other people – helping them to understand something they did not know before.

What is your cup of tea?

This might not sound like fun to you and that might be because we share different values. Some people would enjoy staying home with close family, and others would love to shop for fast cars or the latest technology.

I am not excited by material possessions (I see them as a bad investment, boring I know). However, memories last a lifetime and everything I do creates fantastic memories even when buying properties on a rainy day. Although, I will admit that I have bought my first frivolous possession – a car. Yes, I negotiated and bought an ex-showroom model to mitigate the devaluation. It certainly is great fun – #FunBabyFun all the way.

In 2001, I left the university to go to the University of Surrey in a different capacity. It made me miserable. Yes, I use that language deliberately. I did not know how to rethink the situation I was in. With hindsight, I can see I was being bullied by a member of staff. My work, which I was always so proud of, was being undermined. I lasted six months – the worst six months of my life.

When I finally recovered and joined the strategic partnership back in West London, I was happy again. I also knew that I wanted to be able to choose how I spent my time. I never wanted to be forced to go to a place of work every day and feel horrible.

In a way, holidays are a metaphor for what I want in my life – the freedom and choice to do what I want. At the moment, it is travelling and scuba diving (amongst other things). Let's be honest, until I have seen the world or I am too old to get on a plane, it always will be. The underlying principle is that time is precious. Choose how you want to spend yours and then go out there and do it!

Why am I telling you this?

Because this is what motivates me – the freedom to have amazing adventures, the freedom to travel around the world to see friends, the chance to see wild animals in their natural habitats, to dive with sharks and to learn about different cultures.

For me, 'every day is an epic adventure' waiting to be discovered. Every day is fun (although sometimes tiring and hectic too).

Goals and reasons why

I can't remember exactly where I first heard about making 'your why big enough'. It could have been at my first personal development event in 2007. I don't think I really understood what they meant. Sure, I understood the words but not the meaning behind them. They spoke about positive motivations and towards (rather than away from) motivation. For example, a positive motivation is saying something like 'I want to be thin' rather than 'I don't want to be fat'.

I won't explain all the NLP and psychology behind it. If you are interested, go along to an event for yourself or read books on the topic. (I cover a lot more of the mindset and psychology of wealth in *Make More Money from Property: From investor thinking to a business mindset* and there are resources at www.TheSourcersApprentice.com.)

To summarise, a positive statement can be a powerful attraction for you to work towards. If you think of 'why' you want to invest, make the statement personal and positive and it will have a powerful effect in supporting you to reach your goals even more quickly.

For just over two years I have written my goals every December in preparation for the next year (I also review them quarterly and monitor them monthly and weekly). Alongside each goal, I have a column that explains or records why this goal is important to me. My 'why' is full of passion, colour and adventure and by writing it down I can't help but be excited and motivated by it.

The 'why' explains what the money will help me to do and how I will feel when I do it or have it. It really is crucial. I would love to record the statistics, but I bet that for every time I ask the question of an audience 'Why are you investing in property?' and they reply with an answer that is about the cash or about doing it for someone else, they are not as successful as either they would like to be or could be. Just my unempirical research from speaking to people...

All I can ever hope to do in this book is to share with you my experiences. What I do is not unique; in fact, I would not hesitate to say that every successful investor (or business person) has written powerful goals that shape their progress each day – that guide them towards the outcomes they want to achieve.

I am also not perfect and I have days when I am not as efficient or as focused as others. This is why I have a coach who I speak to regularly to make sure I do stay on track or get help if I am stuck. This brings us full circle to the philosophy of Jeff Olson, who I mentioned in Chapter 1. Every day I make the right choice and take another step towards my goals.

Longer term financial plans: 2013 and onwards...

It's great to have the opportunity to look back and review what you have said about your goals in the past. In a video for the Berkshire Property Meet in 2010, I said I didn't want to run a business. That's now not true, but by saying it I have been able to review and refine my thoughts.

As you know, property investment generates money for me in three ways:

- First, as I buy a property I am either buying immediate equity (by negotiating a price lower than the current market value) or I am planning to enhance the value of the property through refurbishment or redevelopment works.

- Second, I receive ongoing cashflow from my investment, making money for very little effort. I just have to monitor my letting agent to make sure all my properties are fully let, and that the rents are collected on time.

- Third, property historically increases in value every 7–10 years (you must have heard that so many times). I do not count this as a guarantee, nor am I relying on the increase in value. However, research shows me that there is a very good chance that my properties will increase still further in value. If I ever need to generate more cash, then I can either remortgage or sell some of my portfolio.

Alongside the traditional buy-to-let strategy, I occasionally look for property that I can buy, renovate and sell on quickly for an immediate cash profit.

A large part of my business now is finding properties for clients, so that they can have cashflowing portfolios without the work. I do all their negotiations and project management for which I charge a fee. In effect, I exchange my time for cash, which creates an ongoing 'wage'. I choose to do this with clients whom I like and when I want to 'work'.

I also spend time with clients who want me to help them learn to become a professional investor in their own right, offering coaching and mentorships. This, again, is like a 'wage' as I exchange my time for money.

Another way I create income, and ultimately a lifestyle that is financially free and independent, is through helping new and experienced investors develop their personal investment plans. Becoming completely clear about why they are investing in property – what they want to achieve and how they are going to achieve it. This has worked for new investors and clients with established portfolios. We effectively work together and create a business plan.

My immediate plan for the next two years is to focus on achieving the quantifiable goals I have set myself for my business. I have targets set for the 'wages' (time exchanged for cash income), which I can generate through strategic business planning sessions, sourcing and project managing the purchase of cashflowing properties for clients, and mentoring clients who want to become more successful in their own businesses by increasing their accountability.

I will continue to buy investment properties using the strategies described in this book. Primarily, my attention is and always will be on investing in property. As my portfolio of clients with cash to invest grows, I will be able to offer them a choice of rates above the bank's interest to 'borrow' their money or offer them my project management skills to help them invest their capital into a cashflowing property portfolio of their own, depending on their personal goals.

Building a bigger business

I am definitely not planning any more forays into multi-level marketing and, if you hear me say I am, please come and kick me in the shins! Hard!

Focus is my secret weapon – the way to find the easier path to financial freedom. Why would I want to get off?

I explain my businesses in more detail on page 167-169, but they are all about property: property investment, property mentoring, developing property business plans and strategies. In May 2012, Deena, Louise and I started our own property event with a difference – http://LondonPropertyConnection.com

And of course more books...

How is this growing a bigger business? Because as I do more and I am joined by more business partners, I can generate more income for no extra time – as each business is shared time and shared income – but that leverage results in a situation where 2 + 2 really does equal 7.

I just love it, love it, love it

Networking and speaking events will continue to provide me with opportunities to both share my experiences and attract new clients and investors. I love meeting people and property networking events are almost becoming part of my social life, not surprising really when property investment is such an integral part of my life. It is not like having a job; I am truly the master of my own destiny. Every decision I make, every action I take (sounds like lyrics to a song – ha ha!) contribute towards my success and the guarantee of a future full of fun, friends, adventures and excitement. Who could ask for more?

I would like to ask a couple of favours...

First, if you have enjoyed reading this book and found it valuable, then please tell other people about it and direct them to www. ThePropertyMermaid.com and subscribe to receive my newsletter.

Second, if you would like to leave a comment about the book, then please do so: either on my Facebook page, the book's group page or, if you really like it, on both. And of course an Amazon review would be like a gold star!

Third, if you know of other ways to use other people's money to invest in property, please share this information on the group page – let's spread the word and share ideas. If we can reduce our reliance on banks and their lending – show them that we are professional and expert at what we do – then maybe we can encourage them to offer better terms for professional investors rather than penalise them.

Final thanks

I started by acknowledging all the people who have supported, contributed and worked with me to make this second edition of *Using Other People's Money: How to invest in property*, possible. It is only right and proper that I finish that way too.

I won't name them all again individually, but I will mention Liz Harwood and Sue Richardson – two fabulous ladies that helped my produce the first and second editions of this book. Then I just want to say that every one of you has been such a huge support and an inspiration in one way or another. I am eternally grateful and honoured to know you. Many of you have become friends through the process, and many are friends from the beginning – I hope we will stay friends and supporters for years to come.

I would also like to say thank you to *you*, the reader. I am honoured that you are reading my words and are interested in my experiences.

I look forward to meeting some of you and reading your feedback and thoughts on the book page on Facebook. (If you don't have an account, do get one.)

If you prefer, you can email me directly at the address below.

I look forward to hearing from you. Once again, thank you.

Vicki Wusche

The Property Mermaid

vicki@thepropertymermaid.com

Glossary

Amortization: a commercial lending term meaning the loan 'capital' will be repaid over a specific time period, unlike interest-only mortgages where only the interest is repaid and the initial loan borrowed is still outstanding at the end of the time period.

Annual net income: rent (minus costs such as letting agent fee and insurance) divided by the total amount of money invested into a deal including all buying costs (like solicitor fees, surveys, etc). Personally, I would want to receive at least 5% more than I could if I just left my money in a normal safe bank account. My properties regularly achieve 10–14% ROI.

Asset: an investment that generates a profit – puts cash in your pocket.

AST: an assured shorthold tenancy agreement – a contract between landlord and tenant explaining responsibilities and duties. Usually written for a period of six months, though can be longer.

Bad debt: a loan of some form to purchase a product or service that either immediately loses value (e.g. a new car is worth less the minute you drive it off the forecourt) or continues to cost you money (e.g. buying an item using a credit card and not clearing the bill so that the item then costs 20%+ each month).

Base rate: the rate of interest set by the Bank of England on a monthly basis, by which our whole economy is effectively governed. This is a fiscal tool used to control inflation or stimulate the economy.

Blog (or blogging): a website designed to be regularly updated with news and/or views. Blogging is the process or writing stories and articles that are regularly posted to the blog.

BMV (below market value): a specific term meaning a strategy that relies on getting a specific property valuation at a point in the future, to enable all capital invested in a purchase to be recouped or released.

Bridging finance: a specific source of secured funding that some investors use to fund certain deals that require a quicker remortgage or are not eligible for mortgaging. This is an expensive source of funding and requires specialist advice.

Buy-to-let (B2L): the process of buying a property with the intention of renting it to a third party to make a profit from the rent paid.

Coverage: a term used by lenders relating to the percentage of the mortgage cost that is covered by the rental income. Typically 125%: the lender would want your prospective rental income to be at least £125 for every £100 of expected mortgage repayment cost. This figure is set to allow for additional costs to the property such as letting agent fees, insurance, maintenance and void costs. It is a measure of affordability.

Credit scores: a system used by credit-rating agencies. They calculate and attach a numerical value to you based on the risk you pose to lenders. The higher the score (top score 999), the better potential client you are. The lower the score, the worse risk you present to a lender. The risk is whether you will default on your payments.

DIP (decision in principle, also known as agreement in principle): the first stage of the buy-to-let mortgage application process. The lender will assess in broad terms whether or not they want to lend to you as an individual, based on an outline of the loan requirement. They use basic information from an initial application submitted by your mortgage broker and a credit check. The next stage is a full application form and survey.

EPC (energy performance certificate): legal requirement on any property being sold or rented.

ERC (early redemption charge): liable if you redeem a mortgage sooner than an agreed date.

Facebook: an online social network site that many investors use as a business tool, providing sources of information, leads, news and self-promotion

Financial association: the linking of two or more people through the credit reports because of shared borrowing. So a husband and wife, or partners will have a financial association if they both have their names on a mortgage. This financial association stays with you even after the loan is cleared. If one party has a poor credit history, this can reflect on your credit scores.

Financial statement: this is not a bank statement; this shows your total assets, your liabilities, your income and expenses.

Flipping: to buy a house with the intention of selling it on quickly for a profit. So, to buy it and then flip it back on to the market for sale at a higher price. Another term is 'buy-to-sell', meaning the same principle strategy.

Gearing: a term that states how much you have actually borrowed, particularly on unsecured lending like credit cards, against how much available credit you have. Add up the total debt on all of your credit cards and divide it by the total of all your credit limits. This gives you a percentage – you want your gearing ratio (percentage) to be as low as possible.

Good debt: a term to describe 'borrowing' for the purposes of cashflow. In other words, a 'good debt' is one that puts money in your pocket – one that generates an income.

Gumtree: a catch-all website where the general public can advertise items for sale, for rent or that they wish to buy. This is great if you want to place your own private adverts or look for private sellers.

HMO (house of multiple occupancy): often student housing or professional multi-lets. Each council will have their own area-specific requirements, but broadly any property over three storeys high with three or more unrelated occupants will be eligible for licensing.

Hometrack: an online tool that enables you to search valuation and sale prices for a specific property or postcode.

Investment strategy: this can be a way to describe the type of properties you buy. For example, buy-to-let usually means houses let on an AST or

HMOs. It can also describe the type of investment strategy being used, for example lease options, NMD or joint venture.

Joint venture: usually refers to a business agreement to access someone else's cash for investment purposes – could be similar to a private form of bridging finance, though often less expensive.

Lease option: a specific strategy aiming to control rather than own an asset or property. Popular in land and commercial deals – it has become popularised in the UK and, like other more 'unusual' schemes, it is under the watchful eye of the Financial Standards Authority. Eventually this will become a licensable strategy.

Leverage: the concept of taking a resource and multiplying the effect it can have. An example is buying a property using a mortgage where, for a fee, a lender supplies some of the capital required. Another example is outsourcing where a person supplies time in return for a fee.

Liability: an investment or purchase that costs you money on a monthly basis – takes money from your pocket.

LIBOR (London InterBank Offered Rate): the interest rate that banks pay for the money they borrow.

Loan to value (LTV): refers to the percentage of the purchase price that a lender is prepared to lend. For example, 75% LTV means they will lend £75,000 out of the £100,000 needed to buy a property, and you need to supply the remaining £25,000 as a deposit.

Market value: could be the price a property is offered for sale, BUT is more accurately the price paid for properties. This information can be found on sites such as Hometrack and MousePrice. Ultimately, the price you pay for a property is its market value, even if the house next door is identical and worth more.

No money down (NMD): a strategy popular in 2008 to early 2010 where through various schemes 'deal makers' sought to offer properties for sale for a fee (to them), but no cash was actually required to purchase the house. The properties were then highly leveraged and often low or negative rent producing.

No money left in: a strategy that we all aspire to – the aim to buy a property and enhance its value so that at the point of remortgage you are able to release all of the initial capital that you invested – leaving none of your own money in the deal.

Pay rate: a term used in banking to mean the amount of percentage above base rate that the lender will charge you – in some senses, their profit margin. (Although they may well have paid more than the base rate for the money they are lending you.)

Refurbishing: a term used to describe the redecoration of a property to bring it to the standard required by either a rental or sale market.

Rightmove: a well-known website that advertises property for sale or rent – it can be used to assess valuations and rentals. It is also possible to make assumptions about supply and demand in an area.

ROI (return on investment): a useful tool to compare the benefit of investing in one specific asset compared to another, or compared to leaving funds in the bank.

ROTI (return on time invested): a tool to identify the real profit in a specific action, by including the cost of your time to ensure that a deal or purchase actually completes.

SEO (search engine optimisation): stop now and find someone who knows – this is web and internet marketing speak and involves key words and tags, Google and 'spiders'. (Get help – ha ha!)

Term: how long you borrow the funds for. In some circumstances, this can be limited by age.

Yield: a figure to describe the average return possible based on gross figures.

Contributors

I will cheat and start with our new meeting – the London Property Connection – and then move through the other meetings. I have not dedicated a whole page to Juswant and Sylvia of the Berkshire Property Meet, because everyone knows that it is the largest meet around.

My aim in sharing the smaller meetings is to help ease you into networking in a local and supportive environment where you can make connections and get to know people. The hosts of these meetings are all professionals, as I mentioned, and happy to help and support you as much as they can.

I have a page on The Property Mermaid website that will be even more up to date than this book, as new groups start up all the time.

The London Property Connection

Weblink: www.LondonPropertyConnection.com.
Facebook: www.facebook.com/groups/LondonPropertyConnection/.
Follow on Twitter: #LondonProperty and #PropertyMermaid.

- Who hosts the group? Vicki Wusche, Deena Honey and Louise Wheeler.
- What is the date cycle? Every first Thursday of the month.

Louise Wheeler, Vicki Wusche and Deena Honey

The London Property Connection offers a chance to network with a difference. Your three friendly lady hosts: Deena, Louise and Vicki start the evening with a delicious supper (including vegetarian options) as part of the experience and part of the price!

Vicki says, 'So many of us are always in a rush, so we wanted to create a relaxed environment where professional investors and those new to property investment could come and share knowledge, learn, make friends and, of course, do deals.'

From 6–7pm you can relax, chat to other guests and friends over supper and then, at 7pm, move into the main room where your hosts will introduce the evening and the speaker. By 9–9:30pm you move back out into the bar to continue networking.

Deena says, 'When I started in the property business three years ago I had £100k of debt and knew little about property. I now have a successful business sourcing property for investors and helping them with renovations, selling on or long-term investments.'

Louise's background is in building and construction, directing Melinda Property Services in Harefield. 'I started out in the business 15 years ago and gained a lot of experience managing our small property renovation and building business. Over the years, I have been fortunate to learn a lot from the skilled team around me and have been able to buy and sell property, as well as build a long-term investment portfolio. I now concentrate on my own property developments. Our advantage as a letting agent is that, as landlords ourselves, we know first-hand about the challenges every landlord faces.'

And you know about Vicki.

Vicki, Deena and Louise have one thing in common; they are all passionate about property and keen to invite anyone interested in property to join them every first Thursday.

For more information, check our website and then book your ticket for the next event – it's a bargain with dinner, tea and coffee, networking and knowledge all in the ticket price – what are you waiting for?

Basingstoke Property Investors Network

Weblink: www.basingstokepin.co.uk.

- Who hosts the group? Scott Rawlings.
- What is the date cycle? Every fourth Wednesday of the month.

'Hi, my name is Scott Rawlings and I run the Basingstoke PIN meeting.

Scott Rawlings, Basingstoke PIN

I'll come back to property in a minute, but my background is in financial planning. I have been an IFA for over 11 years and, during that time, have helped many clients with their planning and mortgage needs. I am one of the few IFAs who sees property as an excellent vehicle, be it for retirement income, wealth creation or as a 'real job' alternative. In the past 11 years, I have probably helped over 1,000 people in property, whether it be facilitating their first mortgage or helping to design a strategy for their future purchases.

I have been personally investing in property since 2004 and I'll freely admit to making mistakes along the way, but I am now keen to help others and ensure the same mistakes aren't made. My goal with the Basingstoke PIN is to create a successful Hampshire-based networking/learning event where we can all draw from each other's experiences and not forgetting do some amazing property deals. I currently have a large network of local Basingstoke investors and businesses and, as your network is your net worth, I would like that to increase.

So, all that's left for me to say is I look forward to seeing/working/networking with you at the next Basingstoke PIN meeting.'

Harlow Property Network (HPN)

Weblink: www.meetup.com/
HarlowPropertyNetwork.
Facebook: www.facebook.com/HarlowPropNet.
Twitter: @HarlowPropNet.
Email: HPN@garymshaw.co.uk.

- Who hosts the group? Gary M. Shaw and Natasha Caton.
- What is the date cycle? Every third Wednesday of the month.

Gary Shaw

Gary is a property investor, public speaker and success coach. His passion is to help people reach their full potential and attain the lives of financial freedom that they so rightly deserve. Natasha utilises her property knowledge to help organise other property investors so they can grow and develop – from their book-keeping, operational systems for portfolios to upfront number-crunching and due diligence. She is never happier than when sharing this knowledge and expertise with others.

Natasha Caton

However, the HPN is not about Gary or Natasha, but those who attend and have made the decision to better themselves and to enrich the lives and the future of their families. They only have the best speakers presenting (Vicki has graciously done so twice!), often those not seen on the rest of the property event circuit. Their ethos is to pass on knowledge and experience to people not as far along on their journey to success, to repay the debt

to those who once did the same for them. Gary and Natasha are also always happy to meet the more experienced investors, to share new strategies and help them find other ways to improve their existing businesses. They constantly remember that a positive mindset and a win-win outlook in life is really the only way forward.

Humber Property Network

Weblink: www.humberpropertynetwork.co.uk.
Facebook: www.fb.com/humberpropertynetwork.
Twitter: @humbernetwork.

Robin Shaw

- Who hosts the group? Robin Shaw.
- What is the date cycle? Every third Monday of the month.

Robin Shaw is a Hull-based investor and marketeer. Marketing director of Investment Property Partners and author of *From Beginners to Winners*, a book that aims to inspire people to change their life through property investing. Passionate about property and helping people make money with property, the stock market and internet. Robin also runs the Wild Catz Investment Club, which helps people trade options. For more information, visit: www.robin-shaw.com.

Who comes to Humber Property Network?

Out-of-town investors, local investors, business owners looking to build portfolios, builders, mortgage brokers, letting agents, estate agents and first-time investors.

The Humber Property Network is a friendly, relaxed, positive spirited event with a different speaker to educate on specific aspects of property, mindset

or general business. Members network afterwards to share and solve each other's problems and find joint venture partners. It's a little monthly boost to keep you motivated. Remember, your net worth is linked to your network.

Ipswich Property Network (IPN)

Weblink: www.ipswichpropertynetwork.co.uk.
Facebook: www.facebook.com/ipswichpropertynetwork.

- Who hosts the group? Steve Thomas.
- What is the date cycle? Every second Monday of the month.

IPN is hosted by Steve Thomas, a property investor and financial trader based in Aldham, a small village near Ipswich in Suffolk. Steve's prime motive for hosting the event is to help others secure financial freedom through investments by inviting some of the best property entrepreneurs in the country to share their experiences with IPN's membership.

Steve Thomas

Topics covered have included lease options, renovations, creative financing, deal packaging, negotiation, buy-to-let, vacant possessions and self-awareness/development. By keeping a finger on the pulse of the property market, Steve is able to introduce an interesting and varied programme that meets the demands of members.

IPN was formed in 2005 by Claire Wray, making it one of the longest running property networking events outside of London. Membership ranges from the novice investor, to the more experienced, plus a host of tradespeople and professionals who are involved in the business.

Speakers get to know the group's background, and this also helps develop the networking side of the meetings. Each month thousands of pounds of business are conducted between members.

Guests are given the warmest of welcomes, and the group always encourages two-way participation for everyone to get the most value out of the evening. Feel free to get in touch and come along: www.ipswichpropertynetwork. co.uk.

Property and Entrepreneurial Network (PEN) Kent

Weblink: www.penkent.com.
Facebook: www.facebook.com/penkent.
Twitter: www.twitter.com/penkent1.

- Who hosts the group? Rick Walton.
- What is the date cycle? Every third Tuesday of the month.

PEN Kent is hosted by Rick Walton, a full-time property investor based in

Rick Walton

Ashford, Kent. In addition to being an investor, Rick is passionate about helping others on their journey into property and is an educational speaker. Rick's portfolio and specialist areas include buy-to-let and larger multi-let (HMO) properties, a number of which have been achieved using other people's money by the use of joint ventures. Rick continues to grow his portfolio today, alongside assisting clients in building their own financial freedom via property.

The PEN Kent event itself has been running since January 2011 and now regularly attracts around 50 investors, including both beginner and very experienced professional tradespeople such as solicitors, electricians and estate agents. It is a friendly and professional meeting that allows the attendees chance to make new contacts, ask challenging questions and learn new skills and strategies from the regular monthly guest speakers. Former speakers have covered topics such as flipping properties for large capital returns and alternative investments, such as stocks and shares investing to name but a few. Due to the size of the group, attendees often comment on how friendly and accessible all the team members are and how willing they are to help you move forward. New guests are always encouraged and welcomed and feel free to get in touch if you require any further assistance: www.penkent.com.

Property and Entrepreneurial Network (PEN) Exeter

Weblink: www.pen-exeter.com.
Facebook: www.facebook.com/#!/
groups/152595184767959/.

- Who hosts the group? David and Shirley Harwood, Paula Cayless and Lesley Holman.
- What is the date cycle? Every third Tuesday of the month.

PEN Exeter is hosted by the co-founders of PEN – David and Shirley Harwood, Paula Cayless and Lesley Holman, who are all property investors. David and Shirley are HMO experts, having a large portfolio of HMOs and buy-to-lets with several businesses, and who both teach and mentor budding investors. Paula is a mortgage broker and has her own business specialising in buy-to-lets and has her own small portfolio. Lesley has been an investor since 2009 and currently works in the NHS. She owns a small portfolio of mainly buy-to-lets.

PEN Exeter started in September 2010 and has been growing steadily since that time. They regularly have 40–50 members come along every month.

Surrey Property Exchange

Weblink: www.surreypropertyexchange.co.uk.

Richard Simmons

- Who hosts the group? Richard Simmons.
- What is the date cycle? Every second Monday of the month at the Guildford Holiday Inn.

Richard Simmons has a coaching and organisational background in Olympic sport. He got involved in property via improving the houses he lived in and buying places abroad to escape to in order to break a 24/7 work cycle. Richard's life in coaching and high-performance sport revolved around helping people and getting the best out of circumstances faced. Those skill sets have helped him to immerse himself into the property world.

The Surrey Property Exchange monthly network event was set up to fulfil a need for a property forum in Surrey and the surrounding area, where people could get help, advice and knowledge on a shared and exchanged basis.

People attending the Surrey Property Exchange are from many backgrounds with a common interest in property. Most have a lot of experience as investors and landlords and there are newcomers every month who add variety and a fresh focus. The event is lucky enough to have a number of well-known individuals as niche sponsors – people such as Rory O'Mara, John Cox and Graham Faulkner.

What makes the event special? It is an independently run very interactive event, with a round table two-way format. There is no hard selling from the front and there is a clear attempt each month to bring fresh information and new faces behind it all, so that everyone who comes can get a new perspective on the property business and how to improve their own strategy or business model. There are brand-new property deals brought to life on the screen at each event by members looking to find buyers or joint venture partners, and there is an open forum every month where members can raise queries or problems, with a strong chance of them being resolved by someone in the room.

Bucks Property Meet

Weblink: www.buckspropertymeet.com.
Facebook: www.facebook.com/groups/buckspropertymeet/.
Twitter: www.twitter.com/buckspropmeet.

- Who hosts the group? Teresa Hooper and John Cox.
- What is the date cycle? Last Thursday of each month.

Teresa Hooper has her own portfolio of over 20 properties and also matches property investors with property opportunities across the UK. Teresa has specialist knowledge in a few bespoke areas that offer extremely good returns.

John Cox has a background in finance and insurance and has been investing in property for two decades now, specialising in income-generating properties in Scotland. Having helped purchase over 100 properties for investors who are typically asset-rich but time-poor, John is very property centric.

Bucks Property Meet is known for the round table networking style and friendly atmosphere. It launched in January 2011 and now regularly attracts around 60 property people looking to share ideas and connect to each other.

Typical attendees include both beginner and very experienced professional tradespeople, such as solicitors, electricians and estate agents. It is a friendly and professional meeting, which gives the attendees a chance to make new contacts, ask challenging questions and learn new skills and strategies from the regular monthly guest speakers. Former speakers have covered topics such as creative financing deals and flipping properties for large capital returns, as well as many others.

Due to being situated in the heart of Bucks, the property meet is well supported by many experts who attend and speak at other UK property events – having over seven experts attend the meet as well as the main speakers really does add extra dynamics to the knowledge in the room.

New guests are always encouraged and welcomed. Feel free to get in touch should you require any further assistance: www.buckspropertymeet.com.

Property Investors Network

Web: www.pinmeeting.co.uk/
Twitter: www.twitter.com/pin_UK
Facebook www.facebook.com/propertyinvestorsnetworkuk

Simon Zutshi

The property investor network, founded by Simon Zutshi in 2003, was the first property investing specific networking group in the UK and has grown to become the largest, now with 31 monthly meetings all over the UK with new locations been added every month! This means there is bound to be a location near to where you live, work or want to invest.

There are many benefits of attending a property networking group including:

• Learn from other people's mistakes rather than making them yourself.

• Be inspired by what others have achieved and you can achieve too.

• Mix with like minded positive people who understand what you are doing.

• Build your fundamental knowledge about property investing.

• Learn about the latest cutting edge strategies.

• Keep up to date with the changes in the property market and legislation.

• Find potential joint venture partners.

• Build your personal power team of suppliers.

• Pick up property deals from other investors.

If you are serious about building your wealth through property investing why on earth would you not make it a priority to attend your local networking meeting every month? For some people, the idea of going into a room of strangers to network can be terrifying and we understand that, which is why at the PIN meetings we make sure that everyone is welcome, no matter what level of experience you have, and we endeavour to make you feel welcome and make the networking a fun and very worth while experience.

The monthly PIN meetings run on a tried and tested format, which includes two speaking slots and plenty of time to network in the room with other investors. Each meeting is run by a host whose main job is to make sure you have a great time so that you want to come back again and again. The hosts are all experienced investors who understand the many benefits of networking and want to bring PIN to their local community.

Each month we have different speakers sharing their knowledge and experience on different aspect of property investing.

The investment to attend a PIN meeting is just £20 which is a small investment given the massive value you will gain. We are so confident that you will gain massive benefit by attending that we want to make it a "no brainer" for you. If you have never been to a PIN meeting, as a reader of this book we would like you to come and try a PIN meeting as our guest.

All you have to do to claim this £20 gift from PIN and Vicki is as follows:

- Go to www.pinmeeting.co.uk.
- Choose which PIN meeting you would like to attend.
- Click "Book using a voucher code".
- Enter name and contact details.
- Enter "Wusche" into the voucher code box - Click Apply.
- £20.00 will reduce to zero.
- Click "Click Here to book your place now".
- An email confirmation will be sent to you.

Happy Networking

Best wishes from the team at PIN

www.pinmeeting.co.uk

pin
property
investors
network

Bibliography

Publications

Canfield, J. (et al) (2009) *Chicken Soup for the Entrepreneur's Soul: Advice and Inspiration on Fulfilling Dreams*, Health Communications.

Dixon, S. (2012) *Bank to the Future: Protect Your Future Before Governments Go Bust*, Searching Finance Ltd.

Hill, N. (1960) *Think and Grow Rich*, Highroads.

Howard, C. (2005) *Turning Passions Into Profits: Three Steps to Wealth and Power*, John Wiley & Sons.

Howard, C. (2009) *Instant Wealth Wake up Rich!: Discover The Secret of The New Entrepreneurial Mind*, John Wiley & Sons.

Kiyosaki, R. (2002) *Rich Dad Poor Dad: What the Rich Teach Their Kids About Money That the Poor and Middle Class Do Not!* Time Warner.

Kiyosaki, R. (2009) *Rich Dad's Conspiracy of The Rich: The 8 New Rules of Money*, Hachette.

Kiyosaki, R. (2011) *Unfair Advantage: The Power of Financial Education*, Plata Publishing.

Maxwell, J. C. (2007) *The 21 Irrefutable Laws of Leadership: Follow Them and People Will Follow You*, Thomas Nelson.

Olson, J. (2005) *The Slight Edge: Turning Simple Disciplines into Massive Success*, Momentum Media.

Redfield, J. (1994) *The Celestine Prophecy*, Bantam.

Rohn, J. (1993) *The Art of Exceptional Living* [Audiobook], Nightingale Conant.

Singer, B. (2008) *Little Voice Mastery: How to Win the War Between Your Ears in 30 Seconds or Less and Have an Extraordinary Life*, Xcel Holdings.

Trump, D. and Kiyosaki, R. (2006) *Why We Want You to Be Rich: Two Men – One Message*, Rich Press.

Upton, D. (2009) *Create Your Desires and Fulfill Your Dreams*, UK, unpublished manuscript.

Weerasinghe, R. Dr (2011) *Turning Point: A 6 Step Process for Transforming Your Life*, Ecademy Press.

Wusche, V. (2012) *Make More Money from Property: From investor thinking to a business mindset*, SRA Books.

Weblinks to Vicki Wusche

Ecademy: www.ecademy.com/user/vickiwusche

LinkedIn: www.linkedin.com/pub/vicki-wusche/21/494/4a2

You Tube: www.youtube.com/thepropertymermaid

Flickr: www.flickr.com/photos/thepropertymermaid

Facebook: www.facebook.com/VickiWusche

Twitter: www.twitter.com/PropertyMermaid

Moving forward...

Programmes, products and services

I believe it is my purpose in life to share knowledge and, in doing so, inspire and educate people so that they can identify and leverage their previously untapped personal resources. Together, we will create generations of financially secure business owners and property investors and turn our economy back from recession.

I have the writing bug and I will continue to create a variety of books, blogs, products, services and events.

You will find many free resources on my websites, including a free newsletter focused on financial news, property investment and wealth creation.

Visit: http://ThePropertyMermaid.com and www.TheSourcersApprentice.com

Vicki Wusche

Since 1994, Vicki has shared her knowledge and understanding of all things entrepreneurial, wealth and personal development. She has trained or spoken in front of thousands of people across the UK.

During her time working at a high level to influence education policy and teaching, Vicki worked with inspirational entrepreneurs at the cutting edge of a new media revolution, while at the same time supporting some of the most deprived people in London through her work as director for two charitable organisations focused on regeneration, housing, refugees, employment and reinspiring young people.

Throughout her time working in education, and more recently in property investment and wealth creation, Vicki has constantly studied both formally and informally the great minds, concepts and strategies vital to business success. This has led to a Master's Degree, a Diploma in Higher Education and a Master NLP qualification to mention but a few.

In 2006, Vicki was made redundant and decided to step out as a full-time consultant, after working almost a year on a freelance basis. This presented its own challenge and led her, again, to immerse herself in self-development, which she now points to as the reason for her success.

During 2007, Vicki's attitude towards money changed dramatically as she recognised the power of leverage, the value of her time and how to maximise the return on her investments. Armed with this new understanding in 2008, what seemed an easy process to learn the mechanics of property investing was, again, an interesting experience, as challenge after challenge presented itself as she identified and 'tried' to buy investment properties.

January 2009 saw a dramatic turning point as Vicki recognised she either was going to make a success of property investing or find a job stacking shelves! The next 12 months saw her buy on average of one to two properties per month and start her sourcing business. By 2010, Vicki's desire to share her knowledge and understanding of property investing and using other people's money led her to publish the first edition of this book.

March 2012 was a time to celebrate the launch of *Make More Money from Property: From investor thinking to a business mindset,* Vicki's eagerly awaited second book. Vicki freely admits she now has the writing bug and

is in the process of writing her third, fourth and fifth books.

Throughout her employment and entrepreneurial endeavours, the driving forces behind Vicki are her family and her desire to help others maximise the resources they have, whether they are mental, emotional, financial or physical.

Combining all her skills and experience, with an ability to translate complex concepts with passion into every day practicalities, Vicki is focused on building property portfolios for clients who have access to financial resources. Vicki's clients recognise that this is a once in a generation opportunity to build long-lasting financial security for their families and to secure and leverage their hard-earned wages before inflation erodes them. The clients, however, simply lack the time to take advantage – that's where Vicki's experience and service comes into play.

Together with her business partners, Vicki offers a range of support for those looking to build their own business in property or expand their commercial businesses.

The Property Sourcers

- Do you want to get paid to live in your home?
- Do you want 14%[7] interest on your money guaranteed?

For those of you who are asset or equity rich but time poor, this is your opportunity to build wealth! After experiencing a personalised strategy session, your financial and investment plan will be clearly defined. Depending on your circumstances, personal choice and financial situation, we can take the hard work out of investing for you. We will produce and fully micro-manage an investment portfolio strategy on your behalf, which will allow you to reap the benefits and financial rewards without the effort!

the *Property* sourcers
creating your property nest egg

Since 2009, Vicki has been using her experience and knowledge of the property market to build cashflowing property portfolios for bespoke clients.

Offering ROI of over 10%[7], the properties that Vicki sources are identified to generate cashflow and create financial security for clients, leaving them to focus on their lives.

During 2011, Vicki has been able to secure access to a unique investment opportunity and, together with her contractors, can now also provide guaranteed high returns of 14–25% for specific clients who meet the investment criteria. Investment opportunities start as low as £30,000 per property and average £55,000 per property.

The process will start with you working together to develop your personal investment plan in a one-to-one strategy session. During two and a half hours, Vicki works with you to help you recognise the pros and cons of

---

7   Interest rates, ROIs and guarantees are property specific and subject to your personal financial circumstances.

property investment, recognise your personal investment goals and identify a clear investment strategy. While the majority of clients (over 80%) go on to invest with Vicki, this is not a sales pitch. You will leave with a clear investment strategy that enables you to make the right investment choices, at the right time, for you.

With the development of The Property Sourcers, Vicki and Loran can now work with a discrete group of cash-rich investors offering a hands-free process designed to balance the investor's needs for security and flexibility with a busy life. They aim to place just 20 of these unique properties over the next 12 months with a further 30 traditional buy-to-let properties.

This service is not for everyone; clients will need to pass credit checks, have a provable income and have access to financial resources. Professional advice will be provided throughout the process through a team of experts in the property, tax and financial world.

With lending criteria becoming increasingly challenging, please contact Vicki and her team to arrange a free, no-obligation call to assess whether this programme suits your needs and circumstances and takes away your worries and concerns. Then book your strategy session to determine your Readiness to Invest.

For further information on this service, visit www.ThePropertySourcers. com or email Hannah at info@thepropertysourcers.co.uk to arrange your personalised 'Ready to Invest' strategy session.

The Sourcer's Apprentice

- Do you want to start your own property business?

- Did you enjoy reading this book and wish to implement it straightaway?

- Do you feel that you still want even more detail and a step-by-step process to create your cashflowing sourcing business?

- Could you be making even more money from your property knowledge using other people's money?

Vicki and Loran

Vicki recognises that even though she explains the importance of leverage and ROTI, some people still want to create their own property investment business – just as Vicki has done. They have a passion for property and enjoy the houses, the numbers, the challenges and the excitement.

Based on her education, background and experience, Vicki knows that the next best thing to immersing yourself in a live programme is watching and copying those steps in real time through video and audio programmes or joining a mentoring programme.

The Sourcers Apprentice programmes consist of audio, video and workbook solutions to help you rapidly build a successful property investment business. Join us with this informative, in-depth and incredibly valuable multi-learning tool, which takes you from the fundamental inspiration stage right through on a step-by-step learning process to the successful creation of your own personalised business model. Providing you with all the documents, research tools, do's and don'ts, plus hand-holding instructional information to enable you to become a highly effective, cashflowing and profitable property sourcer.

The books, videos and audios enable people to use the learning outlined in this book and in *Make More Money from Property: From investor thinking to a business mindset* and take it to another level. Implementing the steps that

Vicki and Loran demonstrate and describe, you can learn the theory, watch videos as Loran implements the steps Vicki teaches and then hear her reflect on the experience uncovering new insights.

For further information please visit www.TheSourcersApprentice.com.